Pet Owner's Guide to
THE
SHIH TZU

Dorothy Gurney

RINGPRESS

Published by Ringpress Books Limited,
Spirella House, Bridge Road,
Letchworth, Herts, United Kingdom, SG6 4ET.

First Published 1994
© 1994 Ringpress Books Limited.

ISBN 0 948955 44 9

Printed and bound in Hong Kong

Contents

The Shih Tzu combines glamorous good looks
with a lively and extrovert personality.

Dorothy Gurney pictures with Ch. Hasanah No Jacket Required. Owned and bred by Judy Franks.

Acknowledgments

My thanks to my pet-owning niece Christine and her husband Clive Temple for reading and commenting on each chapter as it was written

About the author

Dorothy Gurney has bred and exhibited Shih Tzus for nearly thirty years, and her Darralls prefix is universally respected. She has made up Champions, and bred the top-winning Shih Tzu, Ch. Darralls Felicity.

Dorothy has judged the breed at Championship level since 1978, and has been invited overseas on a number of judging appointments, including the USA, Belgium, Germany and Sweden. She has been involved with the Manchu Shih Tzu Society for twenty-five years, serving as both secretary and treasurer, and currently as vice president.

Cover picture: Ch. Sueman Shihatzu Chaz at Emrose. Owned by Mrs Julie Howells, bred by Mrs G.I. Davies.

Photography: Carol Ann Johnson

Chapter One

EARLY HISTORY

HOLY DOGS

The ancestors of the Shih Tzu originated in the monasteries of the remote and secret country of Tibet. The religion of Tibet is Buddhism. At the core of this religion is a belief in reincarnation, where the soul is reborn in another body after death. It was believed that the soul of a monk, who had transgressed in a previous life, was reborn in the form of a small dog. These wise little dogs were called holy or tribute dogs, and they lived in the Buddhist temples and monasteries where they were highly-prized. The lion is the sacred animal of Buddhism, even though it is not native to the Far East.

It is therefore not surprising that the little holy dogs were bred in the likeness of the Buddhist perception of a lion. Tibet is a cold and mountainous country, and so the typical long coat would have occurred naturally. In fact, one of the Tibetan names for a small, hairy dog is 'apso', meaning shaggy or goat-like. Opinions differ as to whether the present-day Shih Tzu and Lhasa Apso share a common ancestor. There are, of course, certain similarities between the two breeds, but there are also some significant differences.

TRIBUTE DOGS

It has been reported that short-faced small dogs like the Shih Tzu have existed in Tibet for hundreds of years. Tibet and China have also been closely linked for centuries, with the Chinese regularly invading Tibet, and Tibetan kings marrying daughters of Chinese Enperors. In 1645 China conquered the whole of Tibet, and appointed the fifth Dalai Lama as Supreme Ruler. Gifts were often exchanged between the Tibetan Lamas and Chinese Emperors, and from time to time the Dalai Lama gave 'tribute dogs' to the Emperor of China.

This custom was particularly popular during the Manchu Dynasty (1643-1911). The earliest reference to such a gift was 1650, when three dogs were presented, although it is certainly possible that dogs were given to the rulers of China before that date. The most recent record of this custom was in 1908 when the Dalai Lama gave a gift of tribute dogs to the Dowager Empress Tzu-Hsi. It is interesting to note that people who saw these latest Tibetan dogs reported that they were very like the rare Liondogs which had been bred in the Imperial Palace for the past forty years. This seems to confirm that short-faced dogs, like the Shih Tzu, were bred in the Tibetan Monasteries. China also had a 'shock dog', and it is probable that from time to time these shock-headed little dogs found their way to Tibet, and were bred with the native Tibetan dogs.

The first Shih Tzu imports reached Britain in the 1930s.

The highly prized little Tibetan dogs went to live in the Imperial Palace in Peking (now renamed Beijing) where they were known as the Shih Tzu Kou (Liondog). Other canine inhabitants of the Royal Court included the better known Pekingese, and the Chinese Pug. The Liondog was something of a rarity, and considered rather delicate and difficult to breed.

ROYAL PATRONAGE

Dog breeding flourished in the 19th century. The Dowager Empress Tzu-Hsi was greatly interested in dogs, and during her reign she was personally concerned with their breeding and welfare. The dogs were cared for by the eunuchs, and the most favoured specimens had their portraits painted on scrolls. Great importance was attached to colour and markings. As the Liondogs were the property of the Royal family they were not widely known outside the Imperial Palace, and it is said that anyone unlawfully owning one was sentenced to death! However, it is thought that puppies which did not come up to the Dowager Empress's high standards were secretly sold by the eunuchs to homes outside the Palace.

It seems probable that over the years the Chinese changed the little Tibetan to bring it more in line with their idea of a Liondog – shortening the nose, broadening the head, possibly breeding for a broader, shorter-legged body. It is known that the Pekingese and Shih Tzu Kou were occasionally bred together, but one reason for this was to improve the length of the Pekingese coat. There is a charming legend of a pet Liondog, owned by Manjusri Buddha (God of Learning), who, on command turned into a Lion upon which the Buddha would ride. This is why saddle markings on a Shih Tzu are considered a desirable feature. It is because the breed was developed in its present form in the Imperial Palace that it is considered to be a Chinese breed.

The Pekingese, another breed to come from the East, was crossed with a Shih Tzu in the 1950s, and this was to have a significant effect on the development of the breed.

The Shih Tzu soon found favour as a show dog and as a companion dog.

CHANGING TIMES

After the death of the Dowager Empress in 1908, the breeding of dogs was no longer considered important. The young Emperor was not interested in dogs, and such breeding as was carried on by the eunuchs was in a random fashion. They must have missed the knowledge and guiding hand of 'Old Buddha', as the Dowager Empress was known. The Manchu Dynasty came to an end in 1911 and, with the country in the grip of civil war, the Emperor was forced to flee from Peking in 1924. The few eunuchs remaining in the Imperial Palace continued to breed dogs until 1928.

By the early 1930s, dog shows were being organised in Peking and Shanghai, and the Shih Tzu was fast becoming a popular show dog. Sadly, the Japanese invasion in 1937 put a stop to dog showing. The final blow came in 1949 when the Chinese Communist Party came to power, and ordered the destruction of all dogs. Over the years one or two Liondogs were smuggled out of China, but they do not appear to have been bred from. It was not until the late 1920s that Westerners really became aware of this enchanting little dog. There are many stories told of the early attempts to procure Shih Tzus; bitches which proved to be infertile, and puppies given powdered glass so that they would die before reaching a new home in the West.

THE FIRST IMPORTS

The first imports to the British Isles were brought in by General and Mrs (later Sir Douglas and Lady) Brownrigg, and Miss Hutchings in 1930. Around the same time Mrs Henrik Kauffmann, wife of the Danish Minister to China, took three Shih Tzus back to Norway. One of these, a bitch called Leidza, is recorded as having been bred in the Imperial Palace, Peking, in May, 1928, and she is the only known export to have been born in the Imperial Palace. The Duchess of York (now the Queen Mother) was presented with a dog puppy, bred from two of their Chinese imports, by the Kauffmanns. The royal Shih Tzu was named Choo Choo.

In England in the early 1930s there was much confusion over the Shih Tzu and the Tibetan Apso (subsequently renamed Lhasa Apso), a breed brought into the country around the same time as the Shih Tzu. Stanley West's *The Book of Dogs* (undated but undoubtedly published in the early 1930s) has three photographs labelled The Tibetan Terrier, but, in fact, they showed two imported Shih Tzus. This gives some idea of the lack of knowledge at that time. It was eventually recognised that the Shih Tzu and the Apso were separate breeds, and the Shih Tzu Club was founded in 1934, with Mona Brownrigg as the first Secretary.

The breed continued to make progress until World War Two put a stop to all but essential breeding. After the war the first British Champion was made up in 1949. This was Ta-Chi of Taishan, owned and bred by Lady Brownrigg. Incidentally, Ta-Chi was a great grand-daughter of the Queen Mother's Choo Choo.

THE PEKINGESE CROSS

A major landmark for the breed in the West came in 1952, when Miss Elfreda Evans, a comparative newcomer to Shih Tzus but well-known as a Pekingese breeder, decided that the breed was in need of an outcross. With the permission of the Kennel Club, Miss Evans mated a Shih Tzu bitch to a particolour Pekingese dog. A bitch puppy was retained for breeding from the resultant litter and four of the third generation litter were used for breeding.

By the time I came into the breed in the mid-sixties the Peke cross was spreading through the breed. One of my first Shih Tzus was a grand-daughter of a third generation bitch, Mu-Ho. My bitch, born in 1963, was a small grey/white, and her pedigree also included two lines to Mu-Ho's litter brother, Tee-Ni-Tim of Michelcombe. Despite this concentration of breeding to the Peke cross, she was not in the least 'Pekey'. I also owned a black/white dog, born in 1965, with Tee-Ni-Tim of Michelcombe in his pedigree. These two gave me my first home-bred puppy, a silver-grey/white bitch. My proudest moment as a very raw novice breeder/exhibitor was winning Best Puppy and Best Novice in breed at Blackpool Championship Show in 1967 – the judge was none other than Miss Evans!

THE SHIH TZU IN AMERICA
Following the breed's arrival in the West, it soon attracted the attention of American dog lovers, but it was not until the 1950s that the Shih Tzu really began to take off in the United States. Stock was imported from the UK, Continental Europe and Scandinavia. As the Shih Tzu was not recognised by the American Kennel Club, these imports were registered as Lhasa Apsos. The American Shih Tzu Club was founded in 1957, to be followed by other breed clubs throughout the country. Eventually the Shih Tzu received official recognition by the American Kennel Club on September 1st 1969. Since that date the breed has achieved great popularity both as a family pet and show dog. In recent years British breeders have imported Shih Tzus from America, and American-bred Shih Tzus are to be found in Europe and Scandinavia, as well as many other parts of the world.

PRESENT STATUS
The little oriental Shih Tzu has continued to captivate admirers. In Britain a second breed club, the Manchu Shih Tzu Society, was recognised by the Kennel Club in 1962, and more recently three regional clubs have been formed to cater for the needs of Shih Tzu breeders and owners. Demand for puppies and entries at shows continue to rise.

Shih Tzus are now well established in many countries. Scandinavia has been a stronghold of the breed ever since the Kauffmans imported their original dogs in 1932. The early Scandinavian Shih Tzus were, on the whole, smaller and more lightly built than the British Shih Tzu. A welcome exchange of stock, which benefitted both countries, occurred in 1959 when the Swedish dog, Jungfaltets Jung Ming came to Britain, and the British dog Fu-Ling of Clystvale went to Sweden. The Swedish breeders have cleverly blended the old pure Scandinavian lines with carefully selected British imports to evolve a beautiful type of Shih Tzu combining the virtues of both the Scandinavian and British lines. Indeed, a Swedish-bred bitch has the distinction of being the first imported Shih Tzu to become a British Champion.

In recent years a number of American-bred dogs have been imported into Scandinavia, and no doubt will be successfully integrated with the existing stock.

Chapter Two

THE SHIH TZU CHARACTER

People are often first attracted to the Shih Tzu by its quaint appearance: the face adorned with topknot, beard and moustaches looking like a small mandarin, or perhaps they have succumbed to the cuddly charms of a Shih Tzu in pet trim. In my case, it was seeing a photograph of a beautiful Champion bitch which sparked my interest, but I had to wait a little while before I actually saw my first Shih Tzu at a dog show. Hopefully the following, largely anecdotal, description of the breed, will give some indication of the Shih Tzu character and personality.

PHYSICAL CHARACTERISTICS
The characteristic Shih Tzu chrysanthemum head, high tail carriage, and distinctive movement, are all part of the charm of the breed. Although small in stature, they are strong and sturdy for their size, and should not give an impression of fragility. The quaint oriental appearance, and a personality which is a unique blend of self-importance, fun and love, proves an irresistible combination.

Shih Tzus are sturdy little dogs, and enjoy going for long walks, but they are equally happy to go on short outings, and play in the garden. Their adaptability to human needs is part of their charm. They have been bred for many generations as companion dogs, and do not have the instincts of some of the hound and terrier breeds. My little Affenpinscher, for example, although a member of the Toy Group, lives up to her Terrier ancestry; she will see a spider on the ceiling, and sit patiently willing it to come down the wall and, if the creature is foolish enough to get within her range, she pounces on it with great glee. The slightest unusual sound in the distance will cause her to shriek a warning. In contrast, Shih Tzus do not usually notice insect activity far above their heads, nor are they interested in distant sounds. The eyesight and hearing of the Shih Tzu are perfectly normal; it is the attitude of mind which is different.

LIVING WITH A SHIH TZU
So what is it like to share your home with a Shih Tzu? Well, they are free spirits, loving their owners, but not slavishly obedient, preferring to think things out for themselves. In common with all the oriental breeds, the Shih Tzu is highly intelligent.

A typical Shih Tzu is out-going and friendly, with a sense of fun and clownish streak. All Shih Tzus love human company and are never happier than when they are with their owners. A little gold-and-white bitch I owned some years ago, actually cried if she was left alone – her crumpled tear-stained face was a pathetic sight. She

ABOVE: The Shih Tzu is a sturdy, adaptable little dog, enjoying both long walks or shorter, less strenuous outings, depending on the owner's lifestyle.

BELOW: This is a breed that lives happily in small groups, but the Shih Tzu thrives on human company and should not be kept as a kennel dog.

Begging is one of the Shih Tzu's most endearing traits.

was an extreme example of the Shih Tzu's need for human companionship, and I have never owned another like her. However, I cannot emphasise too strongly that the Shih Tzu needs human companionship and should not be kept as a kennel dog.

Shih Tzus have a great sense of family, and readily accept other members of the breed as part of their family. An abiding memory from a recent visit to a Shih Tzu breeder, was the sight of my friend's seven dogs happily accepting six visiting Shih Tzus belonging to another friend. Thirteen Shih Tzus of varying ages and both sexes spent the evening together without a cross gesture. While a few dominant males do try to be top dog, I think it is true to say that the majority of Shih Tzus are well disposed towards other dogs.

TYPICAL BEHAVIOUR

The Shih Tzu welcome to family and friends consists of bouncing about on the hindlegs with the front paws waving above the head. A word of warning: if you are tempted to bend down to pet the happy little dog, you might find yourself accidentally scratched by an upraised paw. It is better to wait until the first outburst of excitement has subsided. The majority of Shih Tzus 'talk', and will greet family and friends with soft, throaty, chortling sounds. Strangers to the breed have been known to confuse this welcoming noise with growling.

One of the breed's most endearing traits is begging. The sight of a Shih Tzu sitting upright with front paws hanging down, and big dark eyes fixed appealingly, is almost irresistible. Lung-Fu-Ssu, one of the original imports to Great Britain in 1930, was photographed in a characteristic begging pose. There is also a charming photograph of the Chinese imports to Norway, Aidzo and Leidza, sitting upright with paws in the air. My own 'beggar' sits up and begs for everything he wants. If it is food, the other dogs pretend to be asleep, but, in reality, they watch to see if I weaken and present him with a tidbit, whereupon they all demand their share! If he wants to be cuddled, he sits up and begs beside my chair. This particular dog even manages to twist his head and upper part of his body around, while remaining firmly based.

Most Shih Tzus like to be slightly scruffy despite the attempts of proud owners to keep them smart and well-groomed. Put your average Shih Tzu down after a grooming session and he will promptly roll and scuffle on the carpet (damp grass is even better!) finally ending with a good shake so that the coat falls in a natural way, and your Shih Tzu is satisfied that he has improved his owner's grooming. I do, however, know of one Champion dog who is very proud of his beautiful long coat, and sits with it carefully spread around him.

MALES AND FEMALES

The male is truly lion-hearted and is quite fearless. He is not aggressive by nature, but will respond and give a good account of himself if attacked. Some dogs, but by no means all, do try to dominate any other males in the household. A few years ago I had problems with a young dominant male Shih Tzu. For months he tried his utmost to subjugate two Afghan Hounds! Needless to say, the Afghans would have none of this, and eventually a truce was declared. At the present time my canine family includes two Shih Tzu dogs and they are firm friends. The older dog, I feel sure, looks upon himself as 'top dog' but is in no way aggressive, while the younger has a happy, very laid-back personality.

In some breeds it is difficult to keep two or more bitches together, but this is not usually a problem with Shih Tzus. I have never experienced any difficulties with keeping females. Indeed, some years ago, when an old bitch went blind, her devoted daughter carefully guided her around the house and garden and generally watched over her until the old lady died some years later.

The difference between the sexes was underlined for me at a recent visit to a friend's home. She owns three Shih Tzus, two biggish males, father and son, and a small elderly bitch. Whenever I go to stay with my friend I am greeted rapturously by the two boys, while the old lady prefers to keep her distance, wagging her tail and watching as I make a fuss of the males. This pattern of behaviour has been repeated on several occasions over the years, but on my last visit something different happened. The evening before I was due to return home, I was sitting quietly when the little bitch suddenly jumped up beside me, digging her front paws sharply into my side, she looked at me inquiringly and wagged her tail. Realising that she wanted the same kind of attention as the males received, I tickled her ribs, while she lay contendedly beside me for over an hour and a half. Unlike the males, who charge at me with great enthusiasm as soon as I appear, she had waited for a quiet moment to make her bid for my attention.

PLAYTIMES

A Shih Tzu will sit absolutely still like an oriental statue for what may seem ages, and then suddenly break into a wild chase round and round the room, and just as suddenly stop and resume a statue-like pose. A pair of Shih Tzus will sometimes engage in a kind of ritualistic fight, chasing each other, then rearing up and standing chest to chest, to the accompaniment of huffing and puffing sounds, then tiring of the game they collapse with hindlegs stretched out behind them.

Many Shih Tzus love to play ball games, retrieving when a human can be persuaded to throw the ball, or just tossing a ball about. My first Shih Tzu dog was absolutely mad about ball games, and quite ecstatic if presented with a new ball to add to his collection. He also had a number of other toys, and was very possessive over his belongings. I remember on one occasion clearing out a cupboard, and putting all the unwanted objects in a cardboard box. The Shih Tzu walked up to inspect the box and discovered an old slipper which he had not played with since he was a puppy. However, he clearly looked upon the slipper as his property. He promptly picked it up and returned it to the cupboard. Need I add, he never looked at the slipper again! The majority of Shih Tzus like to sit on the most comfortable chair in the room. So, if you do not wish your Shih Tzu to get on the furniture, it is necessary to be very firm right from the time the puppy is big enough to start thinking about jumping on to chairs and settees. A wide window-sill or table placed near the window is a big attraction for a Shih Tzu, and he will sit happily at the window watching the world go by.

The mischievous nature of the Shih Tzu was well illustrated at a recent Championship Show. In the challenge for Best Puppy in Breed, the dog puppy slipped his lead and embarked on an hilarious game of 'Can't catch me.' Eyes alight with glee, and tail wagging, he evaded the attempts of his owner/handler and two ring stewards to catch him, much to the amusement of the ringside audience. Eventually, he allowed himself to be caught, and reunited with his lead and handler, he showed beautifully and went on to win the Best Puppy Rosette!

Shih Tzu puppies are irresistible, but you must be aware you are taking on a big responsibility when you buy a dog.

Chapter Three

CHOOSING A PUPPY

Taking on a dog is a big responsibility, which will last for the duration of your dog's life. We are fortunate that the Shih Tzu is a comparatively long-lived breed, and the majority last well into their teens. A Shih Tzu thrives on human companionship and must be treated as one of the family. It would be cruel to take on a puppy, and then leave him for long hours on his own while you are out at work. You must also bear in mind that the Shih Tzu is a long-coated breed, and if your dog is to be happy and comfortable you must take proper care of his coat.

You can cut down on the labour by keeping your Shih Tzu in a pet trim, otherwise you must ensure you always have time for a daily grooming session. This does not need to take hours – a few minutes a day is sufficient – but, if the coat is left uncared for, mats will develop and your beautiful Shih Tzu will not only look like a scarecrow, he will also suffer considerable discomfort.

Having decided that a Shih Tzu is the breed for you, the next step is to locate a breeder and choose a puppy. There are, however, a number of decisions to make before you contact a breeder.

Most Shih Tzus like to be slightly scruffy, despite the efforts of their owners.

MALE OR FEMALE?

Whether you want a male or a female Shih Tzu is largely a matter of personal choice, unless, of course, you have ideas about breeding, in which case you will only be looking for a bitch puppy. If you already have a dog of a different breed, it would be sensible to pick a Shih Tzu puppy of the same sex as your other dog. These considerations apart, if you are looking for a companion, my advice is to pick the puppy which appeals to you, regardless of sex.

It is usual for a bitch to come in season twice a year, and the owner has to be sure that the bitch is kept safe for about three weeks, every six months or so. It is possible for the bitch to have an injection, or pills, to abort the season. This is not recommended, however, if it is hoped to breed from the bitch at a later date. A permanent solution for the pet bitch is to have her spayed. This operation should be carried out when the bitch is fully mature, preferably three months after her first season. Bitches make a speedy recovery from the operation, and there are no side-effects. Some bitches have a slight tendency to put on weight after being spayed, and so the diet should be adjusted accordingly.

The male dog may be tempted to wander from home if there are bitches in season nearby, but if your garden is securely fenced this problem should not occur. On the subject of male dogs, please do not buy a male and think he will make you a fortune in stud fees! I can assure you that there is no demand for the services of a pet dog at stud, no matter how well bred he is.

COLOUR

Another point to consider is the question of colour. Shih Tzus come in all colours, and they can be solid colours or particolours (white with another colour e.g. black-and-white). The quality of the puppy should be more important than the colour of his coat, but some people do have definite colour preferences. So if you are quite sure that you want a gold-and-white bitch puppy, there is no point in going to see a litter of black-and-white or grey-and-white puppies.

FINDING A BREEDER

It is always best to buy from a reputable breeder. The national Kennel Club will keep details of all breed clubs, and the secretary of a breed club often has details of breeders with puppies for sale. The canine press also carries advertisements from breeders with stock for sale. However, if you are a first-time buyer, you would be advised to go to a breeder that is recommended by a breed club.

The responsible breeder is always willing to offer practical help and advice to new owners, and this 'after-sales' service can be invaluable to the novice. The breeder will also supply diet sheets and registration papers, so you can be confident that your pedigree puppy is getting the right start in life. If necessary, be prepared to wait for a well-bred litter to be born. There is no point in rushing ahead and buying the first puppy that is available. Hopefully, you and your Shih Tzu will have many years together, and so it is important to go to a reputable source and choose the right puppy for you.

ASSESSING THE LITTER

When you have details of breeders with puppies for sale, try to visit all the breeders before making up your mind. This will give you a chance to assess a number of different litters, you will get a much better idea of what Shih Tzu puppies should look like, and when you see the mother of the litter and other adults owned by the kennel. You will see the type of Shih Tzu that your puppy will resemble when fully grown.

Breeders are busy people, so please telephone and make an appointment; do not just turn up on the doorstep. Pedigree puppies are not cheap, and I am aware that price is often a consideration. However, try not to make your first question: "How much?" This approach is very off-putting for the caring breeder who is anxious to find a loving home for a precious puppy. Be prepared for the breeder to ask questions about your home and lifestyle. This is not the result of idle curiosity; the breeder is trying to find out if your home is suitable for a Shih Tzu puppy. Most breeders will want to know whether there is someone at home during the day to look after the puppy, whether you have a safe garden for the puppy to play in, and they will want to know whether you want your puppy as a pet or whether you have plans to show him.

The puppies should be in a clean and healthy condition, with no signs of fleas or any other skin problems. If the mother is not with her puppies, ask to see her. She may be rather thin from rearing a litter and out of coat, but she should be a typical representative of the breed, with a happy, friendly disposition. Sometimes the breeder owns the sire of the litter, in which case try to see him as well. If either of the parents show signs of poor temperament, remember that this may be passed on to their puppies.

Shih Tzu puppies are usually whelped and reared in the breeder's home, and you will hopefully find nice, clean puppies kept in a fresh, sweet-smelling environment. If the puppies are none too clean, do be cautious. If you are really keen on one of the puppies, offer to buy it subject to your veterinary surgeon giving the puppy a clean bill of health.

A puppy is not ready to leave home before eight to ten weeks of age, so be very wary of anyone willing to part with a puppy before this age. A typical Shih Tzu puppy should be friendly and inquisitive. The shy one that hangs back may be very appealing, but it will need lots and lots of patience and reassurance from a new owner.

TERMS OF PURCHASE

You may be offered a well-bred bitch puppy cheaply, or even free, on breeding terms. Breeding arrangements can be useful to someone with little money, but keen to make a start as a dog breeder. However, much depends on the terms laid down by the breeder, which can vary from just one puppy back (usually pick of litter), to two or three puppies from two or more litters. The owner of the bitch is usually expected to pay the stud fee, and veterinary fees. If the bitch has problems whelping and produces just one puppy which has to go to the breeder, the owner will be badly out of pocket.

There is an element of risk in breeding any kind of livestock, and the novice breeder must be aware of this. I know of someone who acquired a young bitch on breeding terms, and despite several attempts to get the bitch in whelp she proved to be barren. It was just bad luck and nobody's fault, but the breeder then demanded the full price of a show standard bitch from the unlucky owner! If all you want is a nice, healthy pet, and you are offered a bitch on breeding terms, my advice is to

This gold-and-white Shih Tzu puppy is just coming into her adult coat.

Already winning in the show ring, this cream Shih Tzu puppy looks as though she has a great future.

This male Champion is the top-winning solid-coloured Shih Tzu of all time in Britain.

turn the offer down, and find another breeder who is willing to provide you with a puppy without strings attached.

WHAT TO LOOK FOR

If you think that there is even the slightest chance that you just might be interested in showing your new puppy, or breeding with your bitch when she is old enough, then do be honest with the breeder. If you say that all you want is "just a pet", then that is what, in all probability, you will get. A puppy can be a nice representative of the breed, but not of sufficient quality to compete in the show ring. Equally, the breeder may decide that a puppy has faults that rule it out as a future breeding prospect. Poor dentition, for example, is not important in a family pet or a loving companion, but it is undesirable in a show prospect or in a dog that is to be used for breeding.

Some breeders do ask a little more for a 'show prospect' puppy, while others sell all their puppies for the same price. Remember that a successful breeder with a good reputation will not want to see a pet quality puppy in the show ring, and would far rather sell a promising youngster to someone who is likely to show and/or breed.

At around eight weeks old, a Shih Tzu puppy should be sturdy with a firm well-covered body and good bone. The back should be level. If the puppy is much higher at the hindquarters than the front, the chances are that the puppy will not level out. The breeder may say that this is just a stage the puppy is going through, but it is likely that the dog may always be high at the back end. The puppy should have well laid back shoulders and good spring of rib; neither of these points will improve with age. A young puppy which is light in bone, with upright shoulders and is slab-sided, will mature into an adult with these faults.

It should be possible to see if the neck is of the correct length. A short, stuffy neck often goes with upright shoulders, but a long swan-like neck is equally undesirable. The tail should be carried curving over the back. If it is lying almost flat on the back it will never have the desired 'teapot-handle' shape. The puppy should already be showing signs of the typical stylish movement, but do check to see that the movement is true, allowing for a certain amount of 'puppy looseness'. The front legs should not be heavily-bowed like those of a Pekingese.

The correct head adds greatly to a Shih Tzu's charm. A young puppy's head, completely covered in fluffy hair, is not easy for the novice to assess. The skull should be broad, with low-set ears. Ideally, the eyes should be widely-spaced. The eyes must be round and dark, without showing any white of eye. However, young puppies do sometimes show a little white of eye and this often fills in as the puppy grows. The nose should have a definite stop (at the point where the muzzle meets the skull) and it should be level or tip-tilted.

When I am assessing a young puppy's head and nose placement, I always study the head in profile. It usually slopes slightly backwards from the chin to the skull in a more or less straight line. If the nose breaks that line and is visible, I know that the nose is too long. The lips of the mouth must be level, and should not show the tongue or teeth. Some puppies are very slow in teething, but by about eight weeks of age the average puppy will have his first teeth. There should be six incisors between the canine teeth in the upper and lower jaw. If the puppy has only four incisors, he is very unlikely to have full dentition as a adult. Look for a broad, wide jaw: if the jaw is narrow and cramped, the adult teeth are likely to be misplaced.

When a puppy is around eight weeks of age, the teeth and gums should be level. If the puppy is already undershot (lower teeth extending beyond the upper jaw) it is very probable that the adult dog will be undershot. Conversely, the overshot puppy may end up with an incorrect scissor bite. Always bear in mind that the lower jaw continues to grow after the upper jaw has stopped. Check that the puppy has reasonably wide open nostrils: tight, pinched nostrils can cause problems, especially when the puppy is teething. The puppy's coat should be quite thick and rather soft in texture. Slightly uneven markings on the body coat usually blend in as the coat grows, but a particolour should have even head markings.

FINAL CHECKS

Having selected your puppy, the breeder should give you a diet sheet detailing the way in which the puppies have been fed. It helps the puppy to settle into his new home if he is given the food he is used to. The youngster has enough to contend with, without the added upset of changing his diet. Some breeders will give the new owner a small supply of food to cover the first few meals. If, by any chance, a diet sheet is not forthcoming, do ask for information about feeding the puppy.

Breeders routinely worm puppies, but if the breeder has not mentioned a worming programme, just check that this has been done, and when the next treatment is due.

All puppies need to be inoculated against contagious diseases. These include distemper, parvovirus, leptospirosis, and hepatitis. Some puppies are given a preliminary injection at around eight weeks old, while others breeders tend to rely on the immunity the puppies get from their mother and do not start the inoculation course until the puppies are twelve to fourteen weeks of age. You must check to see if your puppy has received any inoculations, and when further injections are needed. In this instance, the breeder will hand over the veterinary surgeon's certificate detailing the injections. Assuming that your new puppy has not been inoculated, you must take care to keep him away from possible risk of infection until you have had him immunised.

The breeder of a pedigree puppy will also supply the new owner with a copy of the puppy's pedigree and a registration certificate so that the puppy can be registered with the national Kennel Club in the name of his new owner. Sometimes the breeder forwards these forms to the new owner at a later date, but in the excitement of owning a new puppy do not forget about the paperwork. Unless your dog has been officially registered and transferred to your name, you cannot breed or show your Shih Tzu. The pedigree is simply a record of the puppy's parents, grandparents and great-grandparents. Details sometimes included on the pedigree are the registration numbers of parents and colours. The initials 'CH' in front of a dog's name mean that the dog has won the title of Champion in the show ring. The pedigree must be signed and dated by the breeder. Even if you have no plans to show or breed your Shih Tzu, it is interesting to have a record of your dog's ancestors.

A responsible breeder will sell you a well-reared healthy puppy, with all the paperwork in order and without strings attached, but there are a few people around who are not so scrupulous, and it pays to be on your guard. Do ask questions – most breeders are only too willing to spend time talking about their dogs. Hopefully, you will find just the right puppy, and the breeder will be happy to be contacted if you need any help or advice as the puppy settles into his new home.

ABOVE: When you go to look at a litter of puppies, it helps if you can see the mother as well.

BELOW: A Shih Tzu puppy should be sturdy, with a firm well-covered body, and good bone.

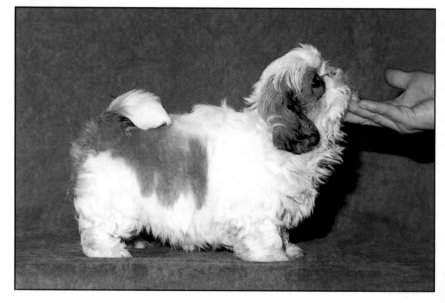

The skull should be broad, with low-set ears and widely spaced eyes.

Check your puppy to see if he has full dentition, and that he has a broad wide jaw to allow room for the adult teeth.

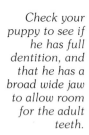

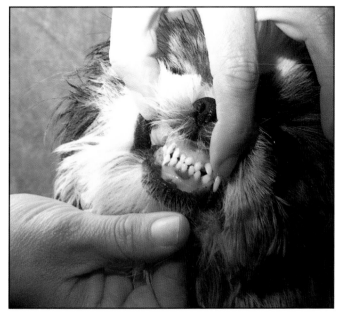

Chapter Four

CARING FOR YOUR PUPPY

PREPARATIONS
Before collecting your new puppy it is necessary to make preparations for his homecoming. Firstly, is your home safe for a puppy? Trailing cords from electrical appliances may well be chewed with disastrous results if they are within reach of an inquisitive puppy. An open or electric fire must have a fireguard securely in place. Remember that anything on, or close to, the floor is fair game to a young puppy. If you leave your favourite slippers lying around, do not blame the puppy if he chews them! Your garden – or an area of it – must be securely fenced. An eight-week-old Shih Tzu puppy is not very big, and can easily get through a small gap in a hedge or even squeeze under a gate.

BEDS
You must decide where the puppy is going to have his bed. Ideally, this should be in a quiet, warm corner, well away from draughts. There are various types of pet beds on the market. Those made of plastic have the advantage of being easily cleaned, but a bored puppy is quite capable of chewing the plastic. At one time wicker dog beds were very popular, and they are still available. However, wicker can harbour fleas and other parasites, and is even more likely to be chewed than a plastic bed. It is possible to get very attractive foam-filled fabric beds and beanbags, but again, they are not proof against sharp puppy teeth.

It is worth remembering that a puppy grows very quickly, so a cosy little bed will soon be outgrown, while an adult-size bed will too big for a young puppy. Many people start a puppy off in a strong cardboard box with an opening cut in one side, and the addition of a blanket makes a warm, draughtproof bed. Make sure that all metal fastenings have been removed from the box before use. The great advantage of a cardboard box is that it can be easily replaced if it is chewed or outgrown. A proper dog bed can be bought when the puppy is nearing adulthood.

It is a good idea to buy a wire cage which is big enough to contain your puppy's bed, with space to spare. Spread a layer of newspaper over the floor, and you have a secure 'house' for the puppy at bedtime or if he has to be left alone for a short period during the day. This is merely a suggested safety precaution for a young puppy. I am not advocating that a puppy or an adult Shih Tzu should spend most of the day sitting in a cage.

BOWLS
Your pet will need a minimum of two bowls, one for water and the other for food.

Feeding bowls are available in plastic, metal and earthenware. I prefer a heavy earthenware dish for water. Plastic dishes are cheap, but they are easily chewed. Remember the Shih Tzu is a flat-faced breed, and so the bowl should be wide and shallow.

COLLAR AND LEAD
Your puppy will need a soft collar and a lead. The collar should fit comfortably round his neck, not too tight, but not loose enough to allow the puppy to slip his head through. Your puppy will not be able to go outside your home and garden before his inoculation course has been completed, but he can get used to wearing a collar and lead in your home, in preparation for his first outing. Do not leave the puppy unattended with a trailing lead attached to his collar.

As your Shih Tzu gets older, you will need a secure collar and lead, and there is a wide choice available. A soft leather rolled collar and lead is both comfortable and durable. The nylon combined collar and lead, with an adjustable collar section, is popular. A light show lead is not strong enough for daily use.

In addition to your dog's ordinary lead, you may like to get an extension lead, which will give your Shih Tzu the freedom to roam about while still being under your control. Choke-chains and harnesses are not recommended for the Shih Tzu.

TOYS
Your puppy will need some toys as he should have something he is allowed to chew, particularly when he is teething. There are lots of dog toys available from pet stores, but some are more suitable than others. You must check that the toys you allow your puppy are absolutely safe and cannot be chewed into small pieces, which could lodge in your puppy's throat.

ARRIVING HOME
When you have purchased the necessary equipment and made sure that your house is safe, you are ready to collect your puppy and introduce him to his new home. Initially, it is best to confine the puppy to one room, giving him time to become familiar with his surroundings. If your family includes children, do make sure that they do not crowd and frighten the new arrival. Most young children love animals, but they can be unintentionally cruel to a young puppy or kitten, sometimes just by loving too hard, and squeezing the breath out of the small creature.

If you already have other pets, the new puppy must be carefully introduced. It is most important that a dog or cat, already in residence, is not made to feel jealous or unwanted. Obviously, you and your family will want to cuddle and fuss over a new puppy, but be very sure that the older dog has plenty of attention too. Cats and dogs can become firm friends and have lots of fun playing together, but if a cat accidentally catches a puppy's eye with a claw, the eye may become ulcerated, so just make sure that the fun does not get too hectic.

CHOOSING A NAME
Decide on a name for the puppy as soon as possible. It is not a good idea to keep calling "puppy, puppy". I know of more than one adult bitch who has ended up as 'Poppy' because that was the nearest call-name to puppy! Try to find a fairly short name which the puppy can respond to easily. Chinese names are nice for a Shih

The great day comes when it is time to collect your new puppy.

Do not be too worried if your puppy refuses the first meal you offer him – he has a lot of new things to take in, and he may not feel sufficiently settled to eat.

To begin with, your puppy will need two meat meals and two milk and cereal meals a day.

Tzu, but be sure you know the meaning of the name. The following are a few suggestions: Kwang Ming (Bright), Fei Ying (Firefly), Ying Ying (Brilliant), Pa Ko (Magpie), Pih Yuh (Sapphire) Chin Choo (Marguerite), Foo Jin (Lady), Chu Tsze (Boy), Woo Pe (Matchless), and Chung Lee (Loyal).

THE FIRST MEAL
The breeder will have provided you with a diet sheet for the puppy, and, hopefully, he will be sufficiently settled to eat a meal. Do not be too worried if the puppy refuses food. Remember that everything is strange and he is probably missing his mother, and brothers and sisters. Try your puppy with a dish of his usual food, and if he does not eat straight away, remove the food and try again later. Do not leave food lying around. As soon as the puppy begins to feel at home in his new surroundings, he will accept food.

It must be said that just occasionally a puppy in a new home will reject the food he has been reared on, and the owner has to find a suitable alternative. However, please do not assume that this is the case if a puppy is being 'picky' on his first day in your home. It is much more likely that he is not hungry because he feels unsettled, and, given a little time, he will be eating normally.

THE FIRST NIGHT
The puppy's first night in a new home can be quite traumatic for the new owner as well the puppy. I remember bringing home my first Shih Tzu puppy, a cuddly bundle of black-and-white wool, looking just like a child's toy. He made it quite clear that he was not happy with the bed I had provided for him, so I weakened and took him to bed with me. He snuggled up to me and went to sleep, and so did I. However, next morning I discovered little damp spots on the bedding where the puppy had relieved himself!

In my eagerness to make my new puppy feel at home I had overlooked two important facts:

1. A baby puppy rarely gets through the night without urinating.
2. Even if I had thought to put down a layer of newspaper for the puppy's use, the puppy was too small to get off my bed unaided.

So take the puppy and his own bed into your bedroom, if you must, but remember my experience and keep him off your bed. It is better to harden your heart and settle the puppy in the place you have chosen for him. A warm – not hot – hot-water bottle, well wrapped in a piece of blanket, will help to settle a new puppy. Another useful tip is to put a clock near the bed: the ticking of the clock often soothes a puppy to sleep. If the puppy cries during the night, by all means go and reassure him, and perhaps offer him a drink. Be patient, and remember that the first night is always the worst.

HOUSE TRAINING
It is important to start house training the puppy as soon as possible. Start by putting newspaper down for the puppy to use, making sure that you keep to the same place. If the puppy makes a mistake and uses another part of the floor, remind him of the right place by picking him up and placing him on the newspaper. It pays to

remember that a puppy will relieve himself almost immediately on waking and after eating, so if you wish to avoid accidents be prepared to place him on the newspaper at these times. Gradually the puppy will learn what the newspaper is for.

After a time, you will want to graduate to a place outdoors. The same principles apply: as soon as the puppy wakes up, put him outside, but do not be surprised if your puppy – with a virtuous expression – rushes back inside the house and uses the newspaper. It takes a little time and patience to house train a puppy.

DIET
After the first few days you may decide that you wish to make changes to the puppy's diet. If the puppy is eating well, growing steadily, has a firm sturdy body, and the coat is in good condition, there is little to be gained by changing his food. However, if you have obtained a puppy without a diet sheet or are not satisfied with the puppy's progress, the following suggestions may be of help. A puppy aged two to three months will need four meals a day:

BREAKFAST: Milk with a good grade of small-size dry puppy meal. Goats' milk is very good. A baby cereal or porridge can also be used, and a scrambled egg may be given as a change.

MIDDAY: Minced fresh meat or canned puppy meat, well mashed up and mixed with a little puppy meal or plain breakfast cereal (bran or wheat). Cooked white fish (do check for bones) mixed with meal or cereal. Approximately 1.5-2 oz meat or fish. A complete puppy food fed to manufacturers' instructions.

TEA: As Breakfast.

SUPPER As Midday.

A saucer of warm milk at bedtime is often appreciated. A complete diet is specially formulated to suit the needs of a growing puppy, and no supplements are needed. If you are not using a complete food, it may be necessary to supplement the puppy's diet with calcium and vitamins – but do take care not to exceed the recommended dosage. Small biscuit snacks for a puppy to gnaw on will be appreciated. As the puppy grows, gradually increase the size of the meals, and at four to five months discontinue the milk meal at teatime. By the time the puppy is around six months old, he should be having two meat and biscuit or complete food meals a day.

FIRST LESSONS
As soon as possible, start to teach your puppy a little basic obedience. A puppy needs to understand the meaning of "No". This little word is repeated so frequently in the early days of a puppy's training, that I suspect some pups think their name is "No No!". However, it is important that the puppy learns to respond to this command by stopping immediately in his tracks, and then you will be able to distract the puppy from chewing your shoes, or whatever he is doing. This can be done by offering the puppy a toy – something he is allowed to play with – and then giving lots of praise. You will also want the puppy to come to you when called. The commands "Come" or "Here", preceded by the puppy's name, can be used, but do

It is important to establish where your puppy is going to sleep and introduce the puppy to his bed right from the start. This is the place where he will feel safe and secure.

keep to the word of your choice. A young puppy cannot be expected to respond to varied commands.

It is important that your puppy learns to accept the constraint of wearing a collar, and then graduates to walking on the lead. Most puppies will scratch and fidget the first time they wear a collar, but if you offer a distraction in the form of a game, the puppy will soon forget about his collar.

Lead training is made easier if you have an older dog, as the puppy will probably trot along beside his canine companion quite happily, ignoring the collar round his neck and the lead. If, however, the puppy is on his own, be prepared to spend time playing with him; try to make the collar and lead fun. The puppy's instinct will be to follow you anyway, even if he does object to the constraint of a collar. A little bribery in the form of a tidbit often works wonders, and in quite a short time the puppy will be lead trained. Puppies must be trained to accept grooming from an early age. The coat of a young puppy needs little more than a daily gentle brushing with a soft brush, but it is important that the puppy learns to stand still and accept these grooming sessions – this will be invaluable at a later stage when the Shih Tzu's coat needs more attention. Eyes and ears and under the tail should be checked regularly to make sure that they are clean.

SOCIALISATION

Your puppy must be confined to the safety of your home and garden until he has been inoculated against the major contagious diseases which include: distemper, parvovirus, leptospirosis and hepatitis. Do not allow your friends to bring their dogs to visit during this vulnerable time. Your veterinary surgeon will advise on the right age for the first injection. This is commonly at twelve weeks with a second injection about two weeks later. However this can vary, depending upon the veterinary surgeon and the vaccine used. After the puppy has completed the course of injections, it is still necessary to keep the puppy confined for a few days longer until full immunity has developed.

Once your puppy is fully inoculated, it is time to begin socialising him. By now, he should be used to wearing his collar and lead, but it is a good idea to start off by carrying him, so that he can see strange places and people from the safety of your arms. Shih Tzus love people so your puppy should quickly make friends with new acquaintances. Do not be in too much of a hurry to make your puppy walk on a lead in a strange place; give him time to acclimatise to a different environment. At this stage, your aim is to give your puppy plenty of reassurance so he learns to accept the outside world in a calm and confident manner.

Your puppy will appreciate some toys, particularly when he starts teething.

Chapter Five

CARING FOR THE ADULT SHIH TZU

As your puppy matures into an adult it is important to establish a routine for feeding, grooming and exercise. All dogs have their own internal clock, and once a routine has been established, this tells them when to expect a meal or walk.

FEEDING METHODS
By the time a Shih Tzu is a year old, he should need only one meal a day, although the total amount of food can be halved and fed as two small meals if preferred – usually morning and early evening. Assuming that you have decided on just one meal, decide on a time which suits you and keep to it. It is not fair on a dog to feed him at midday one day and late evening the next! Your Shih Tzu will adapt to whatever time of day suits you best, but he will quickly come to expect his meal at around the same time every day. There are a number of different feeding methods, and it is a question of finding the right one for your pet.

COMPLETE DIETS
In recent years the complete foods have become increasingly popular. These are produced to a scientific formula, and they are usually pelleted. The puppy formula can be softened with warm milk or water. No supplements are needed with this diet, and it can be harmful if you attempt to add in extras as it can upset the balance of the diet. It is also possible to get complete foods in a flaked form, which need the addition of hot water. Some flaked foods require a small quantity of meat added in order to produce a balanced diet, but whatever form you choose, it is essential to read the maunfacturers' instructions.

There are a number of different brands of complete food, all varying slightly in composition and flavouring, so if you wish to feed your Shih Tzu on a complete diet there is plenty of choice. One very important point to remember is that fresh water must be available at all times. Complete diets are available from pet food suppliers, and most supermarkets also supply a reasonable range of this type of food.

MEAT AND BISCUITS
Some people are of the opinion that meat is the natural food for a dog, and again there is plenty of choice. Fresh butchers' meat is expensive, although some butchers do have packs of pet meat. These days it is more usual to buy frozen meats such as beef and chicken from a specialist supplier of pet food. There is also a good variety of canned and long-life meats, obtainable from both pet food suppliers and supermarkets.

The meat should be mixed with a good-quality biscuit meal. If you are feeding this type of diet it may well be necessary to supplement it with calcium and vitamins. There are several excellent proprietary brands of multi-vitamins and calcium on the market. A word of caution, do read the recommended quantities carefully, as it can be harmful to overdose, especially on calcium.

EXERCISE

All dogs need a certain amount of exercise. Shih Tzus are adaptable little dogs and will fit in with their owners' lifestyles. If you are able to give your dog three or four walks a day, he will enjoy the exercise and contact with the outside world. Dog owners often walk their dogs in a local park and regularly meet up with other people walking their pets. Shih Tzus are very friendly, and usually enjoy making friends with other dogs on these occasions. A walk morning and evening, or even once a day is adequate for a small dog, but remember, as with feeding, do keep to a regular routine. Do not forget to clean up after your pet in public places. Most pet shops stock packs of 'pooper-scoopers', or a plastic bag is adequate.

If you are not able to take your Shih Tzu for long walks, you can compensate by playing games, which are fun, and will give the dog free-running exercise at the same time. For example, many Shih Tzus will retrieve a ball or a soft toy. Two or more dogs will often exercise themselves with energetic games. Some years ago I owned a handsome Champion Afghan Hound, and judges frequently commented on his superb muscular condition.

Of course, he was regularly exercised, but the real reason for his super condition was his daily game with a Shih Tzu! The Shih Tzu charged at the Afghan, who promptly raced off down the garden at full speed, the Shih Tzu waited for him to return and charged again, and off raced the Afghan once more. This continued until one or other lost interest. The game was great fun for both dogs, and greatly helped to keep both in fine physical condition.

A show dog needs free-running exercise, plus road-walking at the correct speed to develop the distinctive Shih Tzu hind movement, and true front movement. The speed will vary from dog to dog, so it may be necessary to experiment initially to find the right speed for your dog. A young dog, whether destined for a show career or life as a family pet, should not be over-exercised. A growing puppy needs carefully controlled exercise and plenty of rest until he is fully mature.

GROOMING

THE PET SHIH TZU

When a Shih Tzu is purely a companion, the question arises as to whether or not the dog should be kept in full coat or clipped off and kept in a pet trim. In fact, it is not a great deal of work to keep a pet Shih Tzu in good coat. All it takes is a few minutes every day. Some dogs do not enjoy being groomed, although most will tolerate a grooming session. When a Shih Tzu objects very strongly to the use of a brush and comb, and it is essential that the owner does not give in and abandon the grooming. If the dog has received gentle daily grooming from the time it was a young puppy, it should not be difficult to cope as the coat grows.

To keep a pet coat clean and well-groomed you need some basic equipment. The best brush to buy is a 'pin' type that has fine metal pins, with rounded ends, set into

GROOMING YOUR SHIH TZU

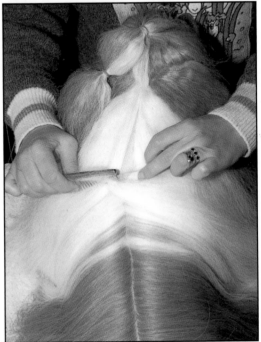

ABOVE: The coat should be brushed in layers, using a brush that has fine metal pins with rounded tips.

LEFT: Use a wide-toothed comb to go through the coat, layer by layer, ensuring there are no knots or tangles. The body coat should be parted along the line of the back so that it falls evenly on both sides of the dog.

TYING THE TOP-KNOT

Gather together the hair between the eyes, and a little hair from the top of the head.

Hold firmly at the base of the head, ready to put on the rubber-band.

The loose hair above the rubber-band is parted in the middle and combed into place either side of the head.

a rubber base. The comb should be made of steel, it should be wide-toothed and of good quality. You will also need a grooming spray (a plain water spray works well) and, of course, a rubber-band for the topknot.

The coat should be groomed from the skin outwards, and this needs to be done in layers. Lift a layer of the coat and lightly spray with coat dressing or water to slightly dampen, and then carefully brush through the layer of hair, repeating until the whole of the body coat has been brushed. Then, using your wide-toothed comb, carefully comb through the coat to make sure that no small knots have been left in the hair. The tail hair must be groomed in the same way as the body coat.

The hair on the head needs particular attention, especially around the eyes. The hair between the eyes should be drawn up into a top-knot and secured with a rubber-band. The hair between the eyes and a little hair from the top of the head should be carefully combed upwards, with the top-knot hair held in one hand, and then a small rubber-band should be placed over the hair and drawn down to the head. The rubber-band may need two or three twists to make the top-knot secure, but it should not be too tight. The loose hair above the band is then parted in the middle and combed into place on either side of the head. Fixing a top-knot requires practice, but it soon becomes quite easy.

The hair on the nose needs to be combed to form whiskers. Both the whiskers and beard can easily get dirty and matted with food, so extra care is needed. The face and whiskers often need washing, and a mild gentle shampoo such as one intended for babies is kindest for such a sensitive area.

Do not forget that the legs and feet also need grooming. From time to time, check the underside of the feet. If the hair between the pads grows too long, this affects the dog's ability to move correctly. The surplus hair needs careful trimming with a pair of scissors.

If you have neglected to groom your Shih Tzu for a time and mats have formed in the hair, do not attempt to brush or comb them out. It takes time and patience to disentangle the hair. Spray a little coat dressing on to the mat, and then gently try to tease the knot apart with your fingers. A particularly stubborn mat may need to be scissored apart, and in this instance, you should always cut the hair lengthwise.

BATHING

If your Shih Tzu is regularly groomed, an occasional bath should keep him clean and sweet-smelling. How often a pet Shih Tzu is bathed depends upon the type of coat – and how dirty your dog gets! Many pets only have two or three baths a year, but, of course, the coat is regularly groomed and the face and feet receive frequent washes.

Bathing a Shih Tzu is much like shampooing your own hair. The coat must be soaked with warm water (not too hot), then apply a good-quality dog shampoo over the dog's body, legs and tail. If the shampoo you are using is very mild, it can also be used on the head, ears and facial hair. Alternatively, you can use a gentle baby shampoo for these areas. The shampoo must be rinsed off, followed by a second shampooing. Rinse thoroughly, and then apply a little conditioner to the coat before giving a final rinsing. This helps to keep the Shih Tzu's coat in good condition. Take care not to get water into your dog's eyes, ears or mouth.

You can now towel your dog to remove the excess water, or you can use a cloth specially made to absorb water. The coat should then be dried using a hair-dryer, lifting the hair carefully with a brush, and brushing the coat as it dries.

THE PET TRIM
The alternative to devoting a certain amount of time to keeping your pet in good coat is to enlist the services of a dog grooming salon. The dog groomer will clip the coat off, give the dog a shampoo, and the owner has a trouble-free coat for six to eight weeks when the process is repeated. This course of action is infinitely preferable to having a Shih Tzu with a long, dirty, felted coat.

I personally do not like to see a Shih Tzu with the head completely clipped. I prefer to see the hair on the head and face scissored to about one inch in length creating a chrysanthemum-like effect. If you would like your Shih Tzu trimmed in this way, have a word with the dog groomer before the trimming gets underway. Another attractive pet style is to have the hair on the body scissored to approximately two inches long, with the head, legs and tail scissored to about one inch. The finished result looks rather like a puppy coat. This style needs attention every four weeks or so.

EARS
The ears should be checked as part of your regular grooming routine. As Shih Tzus are long-coated dogs, they tend to accumulate hair in the ear. This should be gently removed with tweezers, one or two hairs at a time. If the ears have been neglected, do not attempt to remove all the hair in one session, just take out a few hairs daily until the problem is under control. If your dog has a dirty, smelly discharge from the ears, it is necessary to seek veterinary help.

TEETH
Your Shih Tzu's teeth will remain in good condition if they are properly cared for. There are canine toothpastes on the market, which can help to keep the teeth clean, but do remember that a Shih Tzu's teeth do not have deep roots, and too vigorous brushing may actually do harm and loosen the teeth! So use your dog's toothbrush and paste with care. Alternatively, if your dog's teeth are dirty, your veterinary surgeon will descale and clean them.

NAILS
If your dog gets plenty of exercise on a hard surface such as concrete, he may keep his nails naturally short, but it is very probable that the nails will need to be clipped from time to time. This is something you can learn to do yourself or seek the services of a dog groomer. Do not neglect the nails, if they are allowed to become too long they can be very painful for the dog.

THE SHOW SHIH TZU
The owner of a show Shih Tzu must be a dedicated groomer! So do not contemplate embarking on a show career for your Shih Tzu, unless you are prepared to work at maintaining your dog's crowning glory. It is important to establish the hair-type of your dog. The correct texture of Shih Tzu coat is unfortunately rarely seen nowadays; it is strong and similar in texture to human hair. At the present time, there are far too many soft coats about, some silky in texture, others inclined to be woolly. The puppy coat is naturally softer in texture than the adult coat.

If you have purchased your Shih Tzu from a breeder of show stock, this is the

BATHING YOUR SHIH TZU

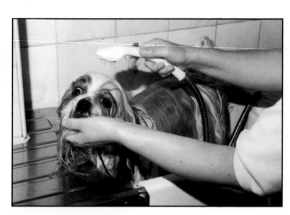

The coat should be soaked with warm water.

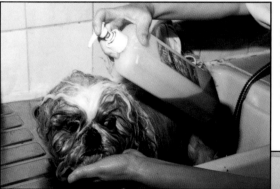

Apply a good-quality dog shampoo, and massage into the body, legs and tail. It is advisable to use a mild baby shampoo on the head, ears and facial hair.

Wrap your Shih Tzu in a towel, which will absorb most of the excess water.

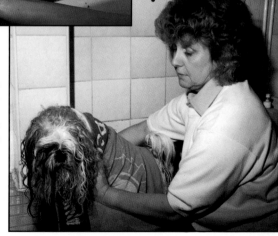

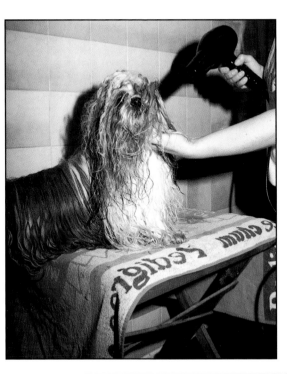

You can use a hair-dryer on the coat, as long as it is turned down to a moderate to low setting.

The coat must be brushed through layer by layer, as it dries.

person who can best advise you on the type of coat conditioner and shampoo to use. There are many different grooming methods, and in the main, they all work.

I use a Mason Pearson hairbrush (bristle and nylon on a rubber base), and a steel comb. I brush a mink-oil or lanoline based grooming spray into the coat, layering the hair, as described in the pet grooming section. I spray the leg hair, tail, ears and topknot hair, taking care not to use the spray on the face or near the eyes. I check that the eyes are clean, and wash the whiskers and beard with baby shampoo. After drying, I carefully comb through the clean hair. The long topknot hair must be tied back, and if the hair is very long I plait it.

This routine is repeated daily. The grooming spray makes the coat slightly greasy and the hair is less likely to break. The comb must be used sparingly, as it is very easy to strip out the undercoat. I usually find it sufficient to carefully comb through the coat after brushing once or twice a week. A greasy coat needs shampooing every ten to fourteen days, and I use a good quality special dog shampoo and conditioner, with a baby shampoo for the face furnishings.

Your dog must be bathed before a show, but the timing depends upon the coat texture. However, the day before the show is the most popular choice for pre-show shampooing. The dog should be thoroughly groomed after bathing, and check to see if the ears, nails and feet need attention.

Chapter Six

TRAINING

THE SHIH TZU'S MIND

It must be said that Shih Tzus are not noted for their obedience! If you want a dog which will slavishly obey your every command, then the Shih Tzu is not the breed for you. A Shih Tzu should be – rather comically – full of his own importance, and such a little character does not respond well to orders. However, the Shih Tzu has a very loving nature and is usually willing to try to please his owner if he can do so without losing face. So lessons in basic obedience have to be fun.

Although self-willed, Shih Tzus are not particularly destructive or naughty, and once trained make excellent house pets. However, a Shih Tzu does like to reason things out for himself. A dog I owned some years ago was a very independent-minded creature, and often caused me problems in the show ring. When the judge asked to see the dog moving, my Shih Tzu would accompany me up and down the ring in fine style. The trouble started if the judge asked us to move again, whereupon my Shih Tzu usually staged a sit-down strike!

Looking at the situation from the dog's point of view, he had been to the end of the show ring and found nothing of interest there, so he saw no reason to repeat the exercise. Perfectly logical, if infuriating, and of course, there was no way I could get him to understand that the judge wanted another opportunity to assess his movement. So if your Shih Tzu refuses to do as you want, try looking at the situation from his viewpoint. My show ring problem with that dog proved insoluble, but a little thought will often provide a solution to a difficulty.

TRAINING TARGETS

The degree of obedience required from a dog depends upon the owner's requirements. My own dogs all respond to their names and come to me when called, they vacate my chair when requested, go outside upon command, walk sensibly on a collar and lead, eat their food together but on separate dishes (I do have to watch one greedy boy), and stand on a table to be groomed. I dislike noisy dogs, so puppies are discouraged from too much barking at a early age. Of course, my dogs bark if the door bell rings or there are strangers about; that is a natural reaction. But I firmly discourage silly pointless barking. My house rules are all quite basic, and easily learned by a dog.

When training a dog it is best to decide on key words which come easily to you, and are readily recognisable to your dog. I always prefix a command word with the dog's name. Hearing his name alerts the dog, and he will listen for the word of command. If a Shih Tzu is asleep or busy with his own concerns, and you call him

ABOVE: There is no doubt that the Shih Tzu is a highly intelligent dog, but this is a breed that does not respond well to conventional obedience training. You should therefore set realistic training targets for your puppy, so you end up with a well-behaved adult who is a pleasure to live with.

LEFT: To teach your Shih Tzu to sit, give the command and apply pressure on the hindquarters.

RIGHT: Always preface a command with your Shih Tzu's name, and the moment he responds give plenty of praise.

BELOW: This Shih Tzu is learning the basics of a recall. When he has learned to wait on command, his owner can call him in, giving lots of praise and encouragement. Remember that training sessions should be fun for both owner and dog.

using a key word followed by his name, do not be surprised if all you get is an inquiring look – your dog will have missed the important command word.

All dogs should be taught at a very early stage the meaning of the command "No". I do not go along with the thinking of some modern canine behaviourists who claim never to use the word. A Shih Tzu very quickly learns what is allowed and what is not allowed.

COMING WHEN CALLED

Always remember that your Shih Tzu will want to be with you, and that it is natural for a puppy to follow his owner. Therefore, it is not difficult to get your Shih Tzu to come to you. Assuming that the dog already knows his name, all you have to do is capitalise on what comes naturally to your dog, and call: "Ming (or whatever his name is), come" or "Ming, here", if you prefer. When your dog obeys, make a fuss of him, and perhaps reward him with a tidbit.

If your Shih Tzu decides to ignore your call, do not waste your time issuing orders to him, or trying to make it a battle of wills. This approach does not work with a Shih Tzu. It is far better to let your dog think that you did not particularly want his company anyway, and the chances are that, in his own time, he will saunter over to you because he wants to be with you, not because you want him to obey!

To teach your dog to go outside, all you have to do is stand by an open door and say: "Ming, outside" and your dog will quickly learn that you want him to go into the garden or yard. To get the dog to return to the house, simply call "Ming, come" or "Ming, here", depending on the key word you have decided on.

CAR JOURNEYS

As soon as your puppy is old enough, start taking him for short trips in the car, making sure someone is sitting with the puppy in the back of the car. It is important that your Shih Tzu learns to relax in the car, and so it is worth spending some time to achieve this result.

It is advisable to get your dog used to travelling in a crate. This is the safest way to travel, and your Shih Tzu will soon learn to settle down quietly on car journeys. A few dogs do suffer from car sickness, but there are several good remedies available. Ask your vet for advice.

THE GOOD CITIZEN SCHEME

These schemes, organised by the various national Kennel Clubs, are now widespread, and they are eminently suitable for pet dogs and their owners. Basic training is given, culminating in a final test when dog and owner pass out as 'Good Citizens'. The scheme started in America, and has been slightly adapted for use in Britain.

AMERICA

The exercises include:

1. Accepting a friendly stranger: To demonstrate that the dog will allow a friendly stranger to approach and speak to the handler in a natural everyday situation.

2. Sitting politely for petting: To demonstrate that the dog will allow a friendly stranger to touch him while he is out with his handler.

3. Appearance and grooming: To demonstrate that the dog will welcome being

groomed and examined and will permit a stranger to do so.

4. Out for a walk with the dog on a loose leash: To demonstrate that the handler is in charge of the dog.

5. Walking through a crowd: To demonstrate that the dog can move about politely in pedestrian places and is under control in public places.

6. Sit and Down on command/Staying in place: To demonstrate that the dog will respond to the handler's commands to "Sit" and "Down", and will remain in the place commanded by the handler.

7. Praise/Interaction: To demonstrate that the dog can be easily calmed following play or praise.

8. Reaction to another dog: To demonstrate that the dog can behave politely around other dogs.

9. Reactions to distractions: To demonstrate that the dog is confident at all times when faced with common distracting situations.

10. Supervised isolation: To demonstrate that a dog can be left alone, if necessary.

BRITAIN

In Britain the exercises include:

1. Putting your dog on a collar and lead.

2. The dog must walk on a lead without distraction; the dog should walk steadily on the left side of the handler.

3. The dog and handler must walk through a door or gate.

4. The dog must be on a lead and ignore other dogs and people, waiting quietly while the handler holds a conversation for one minute.

5. The dog, with lead attached, must be left by the handler for one minute at a distance of five metres – the handler remains in sight. This exercise does require a fair degree of training.

6. The dog must stand steady while he is being groomed.

7. The handler presents the dog on a lead for examination, and the examination includes mouth, teeth, throat, eyes, ears and feet.

8. The handler releases the dog from the lead, the dog is allowed to play, and is then recalled and the lead is attached.

If the dog receives a 'Passed' category against every exercise a Good Citizen Test Certificate is awarded. The tests are carried out by suitably qualified people. Some obedience and training clubs are now training dogs and owners to pass the Good Citizen Scheme, and breed clubs are being encouraged to take part. Taking part in this scheme should ensure a well-behaved pet, and also, of course, the satisfaction of winning a certificate.

TRAINING CLASSES

Obedience classes are held in most towns, and you may wish to take your Shih Tzu on a short course of obedience training to learn the basics like 'Sit', 'Down', and walking to heel. Obedience Clubs run special classes for puppies, and also for novice owners and dogs. Specialised Obedience training is quite different to the Good Citizen Scheme. An Obedience-trained dog will walk to heel, sit and stay on command, etc. A dog which is willing and keen to learn can be trained to compete in Obedience competitions. However, Obedience is a very competitive sport, and it

Training sessions should always be short, and you should always finish with a game.

A crate is an invaluable item of equipment, and if you introduce your Shih Tzu to it an early stage of his education, he will soon look on it as a his own special place.

is a quite exceptional dog which gains the title of Obedience Champion. In America, there is more of a trend towards Obedience training with different breeds, and a number of Shih Tzus have won high awards.

MINI-AGILITY

This sport is becoming increasingly popular, enjoyed both by the dogs and their owners. To qualify to compete in Mini-Agility a dog must be under fifteen inches at the shoulder, and a Shih Tzu is well within this size limit. However, some Shih Tzus are definitely more agile than others, and possibly the slightly leggier dogs may have an advantage over the low-to-ground types.

To compete in Mini-Agility a dog must be fully grown – over twelve months of age. It is important that the Shih Tzu is physically fit – not overweight – before attempting this activity. The handler needs to be quite fit too! It also helps if you have a dog with an out-going temperament. There is no point in thinking about competing in Agility classes unless you already have your Shih Tzu well under control, and obedient to your commands. He must respond very quickly to basic instructions like: "Come", "Wait", "Down", before attempting to learn about Agility.

The Agility dog must jump over hurdles and through tyres, scale frames, walk a seesaw, go through a tunnel, and weave through poles, also jump on to a table, and stay in the 'Down' position for five seconds. The experts with well-trained dogs can make this look very easy, but it takes lots and lots of work to train a dog to tackle an Agility course. In Mini-Agility, the maximum height for the table is fifteen inches, and the hurdles also have a limit of fifteen inches in height.

Agility competitions are popular in a number of countries, and a recent edition of the Swedish Shih Tzu Club's Bulletin includes a delightful account of a Shih Tzu's entrance into the world of Agility. The article is written from the dog's viewpoint, and tells how he got involved by watching his owner's big dog tackle an Agility course, and decided to have a chase round the course himself. Apparently he races round the course at full speed, and comments that the audience likes to watch him because he looks like a flying mat!

By the end of his story he had successfully entered a competition, finishing in seventeenth place out of fifty competitors, and declared his intention of becoming an Agility star!

SUMMARY

Shih Tzus are bright little dogs with a mischievous streak, and enjoy making fools of their owners from time to time. So do not be surprised if your Shih Tzu performs an exercise perfectly once or twice, and on the third occasion decides it is fun and games time. It helps to have a sense of humour at such moments!

All dogs can be trained to a reasonable standard of obedience. In order to succeed in competitive Obedience and Mini-Agility, much will depend on the aptitude and willingness of the Shih Tzu – and the patience of the owner!

Chapter Seven

THE SHOW RING

Dog showing is a fascinating hobby, and to many people throughout the world it is a way of life. Part of the appeal of the show world is that it can be enjoyed at so many different levels: from the small local shows to the big Championship events like Westminster and Crufts.

Every breed of dog has its own Breed Standard, approved by the national Kennel Club, and judges are required to assess dogs by the various points of the Standard. To win in the show ring a dog must be a good specimen of the breed, and so you need to be able to evaluate your Shih Tzu against the requirements of the Breed Standard. Even if you do not plan to show your Shih Tzu, it is worth finding out what a typical member of the breed should look like. There are many first-time owners who start off with no intention of exhibiting their dogs, and then get drawn into the exciting world of show competition.

GENERAL APPEARANCE
The overall picture of a Shih Tzu should be of a small, sturdy, well-balanced dog, longer in body than in height, with proud head carriage and high tail-set. The Shih Tzu should look Oriental in appearance, profusely coated, and very full of his own importance.

All dogs should be well cared for, but a show dog must be correctly fed and exercised, and presented in the show ring in firm, muscular condition under the glamorous coat.

TEMPERAMENT
A Shih Tzu should have a happy, friendly out-going temperament. A snappy bad-tempered dog is not typical of the breed. Nervous, shy or ill-tempered dogs should not be shown.

THE HEAD
The head of a Shih Tzu is a very important feature. It must be broad and round, with the eyes set wide apart. The eyes should be large, round and dark. Ears are large and set below the crown of the skull. The nose is about one inch in length, and set on a line with or slightly below the lower eye rim. The nose may be slightly tip-tilted or straight, but never down-pointed. The nose itself should be fairly big, with wide open nostrils. The lips of the mouth must be level, and the jaw wide. The head proportions for both male and female are the same, but the male should have a decidedly masculine (but not coarse) expression. The bitch should look

The Shih Tzu should look Oriental in appearance and be full of his own importance

The pet trim reveals the true shape of the Shih Tzu. The judge is looking for a small, sturdy, well-balanced dog.

unmistakeably feminine. The British Breed Standard requires the teeth to be undershot or have a level bite. An undershot bite is when the incisor teeth of the lower jaw overlap or project beyond those of the upper jaw when the mouth is closed. A level bite, also known as a pincer bite, is when the incisors of the upper and lower jaw meet exactly edge to edge. In the USA the bite must be undershot. A scissor bite, in which the upper teeth fit closely over the lower teeth, is wrong for a Shih Tzu. Ideally, a Shih Tzu should have six incisors in a straight line in the upper and lower jaw.

The hair between the eyes is drawn up and together, with hair from the head, and is tied into a topknot. The hair surrounding the nose and mouth forms moustaches and a beard.

THE BODY

A nicely arched neck is needed to carry the head proudly, and the neck should be set into well laid back shoulders. The Shih Tzu should have a sturdy body, with a firm, level back, a broad chest and good spring of rib. The forelegs are short with good bone, i.e. bone that is strong, not light like chicken bones. The American Breed Standard stipulates that legs should be straight, while the British Standard requires the legs to be "as straight as possible, consistent with broad chest being well let-down."

The hindlegs should be short and muscular, well-boned, and straight when viewed from the rear. The feet are rounded and well padded, and like the legs, they look big on account of the hair. The tail is set on high, and carried gaily over the back.

COAT

To present a finished picture for the show ring, a Shih Tzu should be presented in full, flowing coat. The correct coat texture has been described as similar to human hair. The puppy coat is usually of a softer texture than that of the adult.

All colours are permissible, but the most popular are gold-and-white and black-and-white. However, there are many other attractive colours including silver-grey-and-white, brindle-and-white, plus the striking solid golds and blacks. The pure white solid is rarely seen, possibly because white is the colour of mourning in China. Parti-colours should be evenly marked; uneven head markings can give an untypical, clownish appearance.

MOVEMENT

A Shih Tzu who moves with arrogance and style, plus the correct action, is an impressive sight. Typically, the driving action should come from the rear – showing in full the pads of the hind feet – and should be accompanied by good front extension, with the front legs reaching well forward. The feet should not turn in or out.

WEIGHT

In Britain, the weight of a Shih Tzu should be between 4.5 and 8.1kgs (10-18lbs), with the ideal weight for being between 4.5 and 7.3kgs (10-16lbs). Although not mentioned in the American Standard, the weight is much the same. The height at withers (the highest point of the body, immediately below the neck) should be not more than 26.7cm (10.5ins) in the UK, while in America the ideal height at withers is 9-10.5ins, but allows for a minimum height of 8ins and a top size of 11ins.

However, what is important is that the dog, whether small, medium or large, should be correctly balanced for its size. The Shih Tzu is a sturdy, solid little dog, and should feel heavy for its size when lifted.

FAULTS

Having listed the points which are required for a potential show dog, I must add that a minor fault, such as uneven teeth or showing a little white of eye, will not necessarily keep a dog out of the awards. Much depends on the strength of the competition and the judge's interpretation of the Breed Standard.

REGISTERING YOUR SHIH TZU
The first step towards showing your Shih Tzu is to make sure that he is registered in your name with the national Kennel Club. If you have purchased your puppy from a reputable breeder, you will have been given the puppy's registration certificate, with a signed transfer of ownership. You, as the new owner, must complete the transfer form and send it – with the correct fee – to the national Kennel Club. In due course you will receive a registration certificate for the dog in your name.

DOG SHOWS
Dog shows are organised differently in many countries, but breeds are always divided into Groups for registration and showing. The Shih Tzu is in the Utility Group (which could be loosely described as companion dogs) in the UK, while in the USA and Europe the Shih Tzu is in the Toy Group.

BRITAIN
In Britain there are a number of different types of shows held under Kennel Club rules.

EXEMPTION: The only show you can enter on the day of the show is the Exemption Show, which has just four classes for pedigree dogs, followed by novelty classes (dog with the longest tail, etc.) in which both pedigree and mixed breed dogs compete. These shows are usually run to raise funds for charity, and the results are not taken too seriously, but it is a good way of socialising young dogs and gaining experience in the show ring.

SANCTION AND LIMITED: As their names imply, these shows have limitations on the entries. It is necessary to be a member of the organising society, and Champions and big winning dogs are excluded. The Sanction Show usually has just one judge, and most of the classes are open to several breeds – known as variety classes. The slightly bigger Limited Show includes two or three classes for the more popular breeds, and may have judges with specialist knowledge of these breeds. As with the Exemption Show, Sanction and Limited Shows are excellent training grounds, and a way of making friends with dog breeders and owners in your area.

OPEN: These are bigger and more important affairs, and entry is open to all, including Champions. The majority of Open Shows schedule classes for Shih Tzus, often with breed specialist judges. Breed Clubs also run Open Shows with good classification and generous Special Prizes.

CHAMPIONSHIP: This can be a General Show catering for most breeds, a particular Group, or a Breed Club Show. Competition is at its keenest at these events, and there are usually 150 to 200-plus Shih Tzus entered. The basic classes at Championship Shows are Minor Puppy (6-9 months), Puppy (6-12 months), Junior (6-18 months), Novice, Post-Graduate, Limit (entry in these classes depends on a dog's previous wins), and Open.

These classes are divided by sex. Technically, the Open class is open to all exhibits regardless of age or wins, but is usually only entered by Champions and dogs which

RIGHT: The Shih Tzu should have a broad, round head; eyes should be large, round and dark.

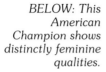

BELOW: This American Champion shows distinctly feminine qualities.

Show training is essential so that your Shih Tzu learns to present himself to advantage in the ring.

have won their way out of the lower classes. After all the classes have been judged, the unbeaten dogs (dogs which have won First Prize in their class or classes) then compete for the Challenge Certificate, which is awarded to the dog considered to be the best of its sex on the day. The best dog and bitch then compete for Best of Breed.

A dog must be awarded three Challenge Certificates under three different judges to gain the title of Champion. It is very difficult to become a Champion in the UK because a dog often has to defeat existing Champions to win the Challenge Certificate.

UNITED STATES
In the USA the show scene is rather different with the emphasis on Championship Shows, both General and Specialty Shows. Under American Kennel Club rules the regular classes at a Championship Show are: Puppy (6-12 months), Twelve to Eighteen Months Novice, Bred-by-Exhibitor, American-bred and Open, all divided by sex. The winners of the previous classes automatically enter the Winners class to compete for points, which count towards the title of Champion.

After the Winners class, the Winners Dog and Winners Bitch are joined in the ring by Champions (also called Specials) to compete for Best of Breed and Best Opposite Sex. If the Winners Dog or Winners Bitch is awarded Best of Breed, it is automatically awarded Best of Winners, but if the top award goes to a Champion, the Winners Dog and Winners Bitch then compete for Best of Winners.

To gain the title of Champion in America, a dog has to win a total of fifteen points, which must include at least two Majors (three, four or five points). Once a dog has gained the requisite number of points for his Championship title, he will usually only compete for Best of Breed and Best Opposite Sex; unlike Britain where Challenge Certificates are awarded to the best dog and bitch, regardless of the number of Challenge Certificates already won. The number of Shih Tzus competing at Championship Shows varies from region to region, depending upon the popularity of the breed in the area.

Other shows held under AKC rules are Sanctioned Matches, at which pedigree dogs may compete, but without Championship points. Societies may also have Sweepstakes and Futurity classes, either in conjunction with a Specialty show, or held separately.

ENTERING A SHOW
To enter for a show it is necessary to obtain details from the secretary of the organising club. In the UK these details are called a schedule, while in the USA it is known as a premium list. Show advertisements are published in the canine press, and it is as well to place a regular order with your newsagent for at least one dog paper or take a direct subscription.

SHOW TRAINING
The potential show Shih Tzu puppy will need to be trained to stand on a table while a judge examines him: opening the mouth to check teeth, feeling for good spring of ribs, etc. The show dog must also be able to stand on the ground in a show pose. The dog must be trained to walk on the left side of the handler, and it is important to move or gait the dog at the correct speed. Preliminary training can be done at

home and in the garden. Ask a friend to help you by acting the part of the judge.

Puppies destined for a show career need socialising from an early age. There are classes which specialise in training for the show ring. These are held in most towns, and are very useful, providing an opportunity to train and socialise puppies, as well as teaching the novice owner the basic skills of handling a dog in the show ring. It may be necessary to ask around to find your nearest ring-training class. The local pet shop or grooming parlour is always a good source of information, or you can visit a dog show in your area and ask the exhibitors (but wait until the exhibitors have finished showing and can give you their full attention).

Shows are busy and noisy, crowded with people and dogs, with the added distraction of loudspeaker announcements. It is often helpful to take your puppy for walks around a shopping centre to get him used to people and crowds. It is also essential to take your puppy for short car rides. Exhibitors travel many miles to exhibit their dogs, so your Shih Tzu must be happy and relaxed in a car. As most show dogs travel in cages, it is as well to accustom the puppy to this form of travel as part of his training.

IN THE SHOW RING

In Britain, Shih Tzus are usually handled by their owners, but if you live in the USA, you may have to decide whether to handle your dog yourself – and many people do so very successfully – or to hand your young hopeful over to a professional handler. These knowledgeable men and women know exactly how to get the best out of their charges, and will not agree to show a dog unless it is a good show prospect.

Even the most out-going puppy can be overawed by the atmosphere of a big show, so try to start your puppy at a smaller local event. If you are planning to show your adult Shih Tzu for the first time, the procedures are just the same – make sure your dog is in good coat and condition, and has basic show ring training before the show.

When choosing a stud dog, you are looking for a male with excellent breed type, sound construction, and a good temperament.

Chapter Eight

BREEDING

RESPONSIBILITIES

If you are considering breeding from your Shih Tzu, do give the matter very careful thought. Do you have the time to devote to caring for an in-whelp bitch, and then weaning and looking after a litter of puppies? Believe me, rearing puppies is a time-consuming occupation. You must also have the right facilities for your bitch and her litter. The bitch will need a quiet, secure place in which to whelp and rear her family. You should also consider whether you have any firm bookings for the puppies. If suitable homes are not available when the puppies are ready to leave home, are you in a position to keep them until the right homes come along?

The stud dog and brood bitch must complement each other in looks and in pedigree

Your bitch may well have a trouble-free time and give birth to a healthy litter of puppies, but it is important to bear in mind that some bitches have problems whelping and you may face big veterinary bills. All these points have to be considered before you decide on the great adventure of breeding a litter of Shih Tzus.

THE BROOD BITCH
The bitch should be a typical specimen of the breed, without major faults either in her physical make-up or in temperament. You must ensure that she is healthy and in good overall condition.

A bitch usually comes in season every six months, although with some bitches the interval between seasons may be longer and, very occasionally, it may be shorter. A puppy often has a first season at around ten to twelve months, but it is not unusual for a puppy as young as five to six months to come in season. The bitch continues to come in season regularly throughout her life. The fact that a bitch is capable of producing puppies twice a year, does not mean that she should be used as a breeding machine. Responsible breeders take great care of their bitches, and allow at least a year between litters.

The best age for a bitch to have a first litter is around two years of age. Please, do not breed with a very young bitch. Remember that she needs time to mature, both mentally and physically, before embarking on motherhood. Pregnancy can be very taxing for the older bitch too. In Britain the Kennel Club will not register puppies born to bitches of eight years of age and older.

THE STUD DOG
If your Shih Tzu is a male, you may wish to consider using him at stud. However, unless your dog is very well-bred and has been successful in the show ring, there is unlikely to be a demand for his services. Stud work is not easy, and the dog has to be trained and understand just what is required of him. If your dog is a nice average male and unlikely to hit the high spots as a show dog, it is far better to keep him purely as a companion.

You may be lucky enough to own a really good young dog, in which case you will get inquiries for his services. A young dog is usually ready to start stud work at ten to twelve months of age, but he should be used very sparingly until he is fully mature. Occasionally a dog puppy will be fertile at six or seven months of age. I remember a breeder allowing a six-month-old dog puppy to live with her bitches, and much to her surprise, all the bitches became pregnant! Obviously a very precocious young man. Be very careful when choosing the first bitch to visit your dog. She should be a mature, placid brood – not an inexperienced maiden. Try to enlist the help of an experienced stud dog owner for the first service, both you and your dog will benefit from the expertise. When your dog is a proven sire of puppies, he can be sparingly used at stud.

CHOOSING A STUD DOG
When you have thought about it, and you are absolutely sure that you want to go ahead and breed from your bitch, the next step is to find the right partner for her. The nice little male down the road is unlikely to be suitable, and the latest Champion in the breed may not be the right choice for her either.

If you are lucky enough to have purchased your bitch from an established breeder, go back and ask advice about a prospective stud dog. The breeder will know the good points and the failings of your bitch's parents and grandparents – and, very likely, several generations further back too – and will be able to suggest a suitably-bred dog. If you cannot, or do not want to seek help from the bitch's breeder, you should find the following information helpful.

WHAT TO LOOK FOR
There are various points to consider when selecting a stud dog for your bitch. The main aim should be to improve your original stock. Breed type (a rather indefinable quality, but essentially it means a dog which epitomises the very essence of its breed) conformation (construction and appearance) and temperament are all important considerations. To elaborate a little; a dog must have correct type to be typical of the breed, and a dog with faulty construction will almost certainly pass his faults on to his progeny. The true Shih Tzu temperament is happy, friendly and out-going – a bad-tempered or very nervous Shih Tzu should simply not be bred from.

COLOUR BREEDING
The Breed Standard permits all colours, but some people do have a definite colour preference, and to breed for a certain colour is understandable. However, colour and markings should not be the top priority when choosing a stud dog. If you are planning to breed a gold-and-white bitch to a gold-and-white dog, the chances are that you will get a litter of gold-and-white puppies, provided that the dog and bitch both have a gold-and-white ancestry. If the breeding behind the parents includes other colours, then the resultant litter may include puppies of various colours.

It should be understood that breeding for colour will not necessarily produce the desired colour in any of the resulting puppies. If, for example, you own a black-and-white bitch and decide to use a solid gold dog in the hope of breeding a puppy of this colour, you may succeed in breeding puppies of the desired solid gold colour, and also black-and-whites, or you could end up with solid coloured puppies, but black instead of gold!

METHODS OF BREEDING
Another point to consider is whether you should line-breed or outcross. Line-breeding is when both parents are related, and the aim is to loosely remain within a family. Outcrossing is when a dog from a completely different line is used. Both methods have their virtues. If you have a line-bred bitch of good type, it would be sensible to select a good male of similar – but not too close – bloodlines. Some stud dogs are very dominant and consistently sire good-quality puppies, even to inferior bitches. So if your bitch's pedigree is rather undistinguished, do not try to line-breed. You would be better off outcrossing to a dog capable of reproducing his own good points. In-breeding, which involves the breeding together of close relatives, such as daughter to father, and sister to brother, is very rarely practised in dog breeding. It requires a great deal of knowledge on the part of the breeder, and should not be attempted by a newcomer to dog breeding.

BOOKING THE STUD DOG
Having decided on the stud dog you would like to be the father of your bitch's litter,

A Shih Tzu puppy at two days old. The pigment on the foreface and nose will darken with maturity.

A litter at ten days old – the eyes are just beginning to open.

Puppies at two weeks old, now starting to take in their surroundings.

Shih Tzus make good mothers, but as the puppies grow they will spend less time with their litter.

you must contact the stud dog owner and find out whether your bitch is acceptable! Assuming that the dog's owner has no objection to your bitch, the next step is to book the services of the dog, at the same time giving his owner some indication of when the bitch is due in season. It is important to make all the necessary arrangements well in advance.

The owner will charge a fee for the use of the dog. Stud fees depend upon the breeding and show winning of the dog, and the success of his progeny. The stud fee is payable at the time of the service, and it should be noted that the fee is for the service and is not refundable if the bitch does not conceive. Some stud dog owners do give a second free service if a bitch fails to produce puppies, but it should be understood that this is at the stud dog owner's discretion; it is not a right.

The situation is rather different if the dog is unproven (has not sired a litter before). In this case, the stud fee should be payable only if and when puppies are born. However, it is not a good idea to put a maiden bitch and a young, inexperienced dog together. It is far more sensible to take your maiden bitch to an experienced stud dog.

WHEN TO MATE

A few weeks before your bitch is due in season, ask your veterinary surgeon to check her over, just to make sure that she is 100 per cent healthy and unlikely to have problems whelping. You should also ask the vet about worming the bitch. It is important to note the first day of the season, and the bitch should be examined daily for the first signs of colour. A red discharge signals the onset of the season, and the time for mating is counted from the first day of showing colour.

A bitch is generally ready for mating between the ninth and fourteenth day from the onset of the season, with the eleventh and twelfth days usually being the most successful. By this time, the colour of the bitch's discharge will have faded, and the vulva will be soft and enlarged. The bitch will indicate her readiness for mating by standing with her tail curled to one side. A few bitches are ready earlier than the ninth day or later than the fourteenth, so it is necessary to watch for the signs.

If the stud dog lives some distance from you, it may be worthwhile to get your veterinary surgeon to test the bitch for the best day to mate her. It is frustrating and expensive to travel hundreds of miles only to find that your female is not ready, and the journey has to be repeated a couple of days later. By the way, do not forget to contact the stud dog owner at the onset of the bitch's season, and again when the bitch is ready for mating.

THE MATING

The stud dog owner will be in charge of the service. The bitch's owner is usually allowed to be present, but if a stud dog performs better without the presence of strangers, you may be asked to absent yourself. The stud dog owner generally has an assistant – sometimes the bitch's owner – to hold the bitch's head and support the body; this leaves the owner free to concentrate on the dog.

The dog will mount the bitch, and once he has penetrated, care must be taken that he does not immediately slip out again. There is a bulb in the dog's penis which swells when inside the bitch, causing the pair to be locked together. This is known as the tie. The dog may turn himself, or he may be helped to turn so that dog and bitch are tail to tail. The dog's owner usually holds the tails to make sure the bitch does not attempt to pull away. If the dog is experienced and the bitch receptive, a mating may take place quite quickly, but the tie may last from a few minutes to over an hour. However, it is not always so simple, and it may take lots of patience and several hours to get the desired result. Sometimes it may be necessary to return a day or two later for another attempt, or for a second mating.

On payment of the stud fee, the owner of the dog will give the bitch's owner a copy of the dog's pedigree, and a Kennel Club registration form. The part of the form relating to the dog will have been completed and signed by the stud dog's owner. A few weeks after the birth of the litter, the registration form should be completed, and together with the appropriate fee, sent to the Kennel Club.

THE IN-WHELP BITCH

After the bitch has been mated she must be kept away from other dogs until she has completed her season – accidents have been known to happen! The normal gestation period is sixty-three days. For the first few weeks, there will be no change in the bitch, and all she needs is her usual amount of food and exercise. Do not start feeding for six from day one! Those early weeks wondering "is she, isn't she?" seem endless. Gradually, signs appear.

The bitch may go off her food about three weeks after she has been mated, and the nipples may become enlarged and pinkish in colour. Thanks to a comparatively recent invention, it is now possible to have a bitch checked by an ultrasonic scanner, which will reveal the number of puppies she is carrying, or if she has 'missed'.

Assuming that all is well, the bitch will gradually increase in size, and for the last three to four weeks of her pregnancy she will eat appreciably more. Remember that she will find it easier to digest three or four small meals, rather than one large feast. A small quantity of calcium and Vitamin D may be added to her food. Many breeders give raspberry leaf tablets to help the bitch give birth more easily.

 Some bitches will take great care of themselves, resting and walking sedately; while others seem oblivious of their increasing girth and continue to rush about the house and garden. It is essential to watch over the very active mother-to-be to make sure that she does not injure herself jumping on and off the furniture.

The Shih Tzu's long, flowing coat can prove hazardous for tiny puppies, and will need attention before the litter is due. The hair around the nipples must be carefully trimmed away to enable the puppies to feed safely. The long body and tail hair should be trimmed quite short, or the hair can be plaited or secured with rubber bands in 'bunches'. Whichever method you decide upon, the coat must be kept clean and regularly groomed out.

WHELPING EQUIPMENT

Well before the time your bitch is due to whelp, you will need to decide on the place where you want her to have the puppies. The bitch will have her own ideas about the right place to have her family – it could be a small cupboard or the middle of your bed! So it is important to get the bitch settled and happy in your choice of whelping quarters.

A whelping box for a Shih Tzu should be at least 24 inches (61cms) square, and 18-20 inches (46-51cms) high, with a safety rail fixed on the inside. This should be roughly 2 inches (5 cms) from the base and 2 inches (5cms) from the sides. One side of the pen should include a door. The top should be removable, to allow easy access

A litter of puppies now fully weaned.

At six weeks of age, the puppies are at their most appealing as their individual characters start to emerge.

The puppies will enjoy each other's companionship as they develop, playing together, and snuggling up to each other for warmth and comfort when they sleep.

to the bitch and puppies. The whelping box should be placed in a quiet room away from other animals.

You will also need a warm, towel-lined box in which to place the newborn pups, plenty of spare newspapers, sterilised curved blunt-end scissors, sterilised thread, Vaseline, disinfectant, towels, cotton wool, paper and pen.

Three days before the bitch is due to whelp, ask your veterinary surgeon to have a look at her. Hopefully, he will confirm that all is progressing satisfactorily. Make sure that the bitch is not left alone the week before the puppies are due, just in case she starts to whelp early. Most bitches give birth on the sixty-third day, but there is no cause for alarm if a bitch whelps two days early or late. However, if the bitch has not given birth by the sixty-sixth day, there may be a problem, so seek veterinary help. Puppies born before the fifty-eighth day will almost certainly be very weak and may not survive, but on the principle that "where there's life, there's hope" it is well worth trying to rear premature puppies.

THE WHELPING
The bitch must be watched carefully for the first signs of whelping. The box should be lined with several layers of newspapers, and the bitch will often – but not always – shred the paper, making herself a nest. The bitch may go off her food if labour is imminent, and she may be worried and restless. About twelve hours before the birth, the bitch's temperature will drop. When the vulva becomes soft and swollen, and there is a discharge, parturition is not far off. The bitch will start to heave and push against the whelping box at approximately fifteen minute intervals. If she has not produced a puppy within an hour of starting to push, your veterinary surgeon should be called.

The first sign that a puppy is about to be born is the appearance of fluid followed by the puppy's head. Another push from the mother, and the rest of the pup emerges. The puppy will be enclosed in a membranous sac. The bitch should remove this, but if she does not, you must wipe the puppy making sure that the nose and mouth are free. The newborn puppy is followed by the placenta, and it is important to make sure that they all come away. The bitch may eat some of the placentas and should sever the umbilical cord with her teeth. Sometimes a maiden bitch forgets or has difficulty due to her short nose. If you have to cut the cord yourself great care must be taken not to damage the puppy. The end of the cord can be tied using the sterilised thread.

The next puppy may follow very quickly, or two or three hours later. When all the puppies have been born, the bitch will settle down to feeding her new family. Make a note of each puppy's weight at birth – generally 4-8oz – sex, colour, and distinguishing markings. As a precaution, ask your veterinary surgeon to visit your home and check that all is well with both mother and babies.

POST-WHELPING
The new family must be kept warm and free from draughts, and well away from bright lights. The base of the whelping box should be covered with suitable bedding. The fleecy, synthetic type of bedding is very good, although some bitches prefer newspaper or even bare boards! The mother will most likely have to be coaxed to eat, and will also be reluctant to leave the whelping box to go outside to relieve herself. When she returns, watch how she 'counts heads', making sure that all her

precious babies are still there. If the puppies are strong and healthy, and the bitch has a good supply of milk, they will thrive and put on weight. A very weak or premature whelp may need expert assistance. Many experienced breeders are willing to help the novice, so try to make friends with someone living in your area (not necessarily a Shih Tzu breeder), who would help in an emergency – and don't forget a good vet is on call twenty-four hours a day. In a small book of this kind it is not possible for me to include all the problems which may arise with whelping bitches and newborn puppies, but there are excellent books available which cover these subjects in great detail.

THE GROWING PUPPIES
It is fascinating to watch the puppies as they grow and develop. At around ten to fourteen days the eyes will open, and at about three weeks the puppies will start to stagger to their feet. By four weeks of age, tails will start to wag, and, of course, the coats are growing the whole time. The mother will clean her young, but you should gently groom each puppy, brushing the coat with a soft brush, and check that eyes and ears are clean, and that the needle-sharp nails are not too long. The puppies will need worming at four or five weeks old.

WEANING
Opinions vary as to the best age to start weaning. If the bitch still has plenty of milk and the litter is contented, the pups can be taught to lap milk at three or four weeks. However, if it is a large litter and the bitch is struggling to cope, you will need to start weaning earlier. Goat's milk is particularly good for growing puppies. By the time the litter is four or five weeks old, the bitch will be spending time away from them, and the pups can gradually be introduced to solid food.

At one time almost all puppies were weaned on to raw scraped lean beef, which is, of course, an excellent food. If you are feeding your puppies in this way, it is customary to give two small meals daily of meat, and two milk meals. As the puppies grow, the milk should be thickened with a baby cereal or porridge. A good-quality canned meat is specially formulated for puppies, and this may be given in place of fresh meat.

The alternative feeding method is to wean the puppies on to one of the complete puppy foods, which can be softened with warm milk or water, and this can be lapped by the very young puppies. As the puppies grow, the softened food is made to a firmer consistency or fed dry. Both feeding methods produce strong, healthy puppies. The pups should be completely weaned by eight weeks old. By this age they should be away from their mother during the day, returning to her at night.

LEAVING HOME
By the time the puppies are old enough to leave home, at eight to ten weeks (assuming you have reared them properly) they will be sturdy, healthy little characters, eating well, and they will have been properly wormed. In the UK many breeders insure their puppies for the first few weeks in their new home. The premium, which covers the purchase price and any veterinary bills, is included in the price of the puppy. The new owner then has the option of renewing the insurance cover. This practice is not customary in the USA.

The important paperwork must not be overlooked. Pedigrees must be made out

A beautifully reared puppy, looking clean, bright-eyed, and the right weight for his size. He is now ready to leave his mother and littermates and settle into his new home.

for every puppy, and the breeder must complete the necessary paperwork so that each puppy can be registered with the Kennel Club. Serious breeders often have a Kennel Club registered affix, and this word is used as part of the registered name of a dog bred by that person. For example, my registered affix is 'Darralls', and puppies bred by me might be registered as Darralls Adam, Darralls Alice, and so on.

If you want to be able to register your puppies with your own exclusive affix, it will be necessary to apply to the Kennel Club for an application form. As it takes some months to obtain an affix, the application should be made before the bitch is mated. It is, of course, in order to register puppies without using an affix, but do try to be original in your choice of names. The new owner should be given a signed pedigree, together with the KC registration certificate, with the transfer section completed and signed. You should also supply a receipt for the purchase price, and a diet sheet for each puppy. If you do not have homes waiting for all your puppies, it may be necessary to advertise the remaining puppies. Do remember to keep the advertisement factual: breed, age, colour, sex, KC registration, and insurance cover if applicable. If you include the names of the parents make sure that they are shown correctly – newcomers to dog breeding often get confused over this point.

Puppies are sired by the dog, out of or ex the bitch, with the male's name first, i.e. Jim ex Jennie. Get this wrong and you are not only advertising puppies but also that you are a complete novice! As the people who answer your advertisement will be unknown to you, you must do your best to ensure that the would-be owners are suitable. Taking care of a young puppy can be time-consuming, so it is essential to check that the prospective owner has the time to look after a puppy and can provide a suitable home.

Chapter Nine

HEALTH CARE

A Shih Tzu is not delicate in any way, in fact, he is a hardy little dog. A dog which is properly cared for – as outlined in earlier chapters – usually has few health problems. A well-balanced diet, regular grooming, and a warm draught-free bed all help to keep your dog fit.

If you have taken on a puppy for the first time, it is important to find a veterinary surgeon in your area. Hopefully, you and your pet will not have to see too much of the inside of the vet's surgery! Prevention is always better than cure, and it is important that every dog owner is aware of the common ailments in order to seek advice before the condition becomes uncomfortable for the dog or becomes more serious due to neglect.

CANINE AILMENTS

ANAL GLANDS

A few dogs have trouble with their anal glands. If your dog starts to scrape his bottom along the ground, and/or turns and chews at his hindquarters, the anal glands probably need emptying. It is not difficult to expel the waste from the anal glands, but I would suggest that if your dog has this problem you get an experienced person, such as a breeder, a professional groomer or your veterinary surgeon, to show you the right way to go about it.

In my experience, the majority of dogs go through life without having anal gland problems, and although I have owned dogs for most of my life, I have only had one with anal gland trouble. There is no need to interfere with the anal glands unless the dog has a problem with them.

CANKER

If your dog has a discharge from his ears, suspect canker and seek veterinary assistance.

COPROPHAGY

Some dogs develop the habit of eating their own excreta. This is very unpleasant, particularly with a house pet. It is thought that this may be caused by a mineral and vitamin deficiency, and there are dietary additives available to help with this problem. On a practical note, try to break the habit by immediately clearing up after your dog – do not give him the chance to get there first.

COUGHS AND COLDS
Although the condition may not appear severe, it could turn to bronchitis or pneumonia, and so it is better to seek veterinary help as soon as possible.

EYE PROBLEMS
Ulcerated eyes are not unknown in Shih Tzus. Sometimes a scratch or knock can cause an ulcer, which will often need veterinary attention. A useful first-aid remedy is to apply pure cod-liver oil to the eyes. Many years ago I owned a beautiful young Shih Tzu who had more than her fair share of eye ulcers. My vet said that the problem was caused by the uneven surface of her eyes, and recommended that I put cod-liver oil in her eyes daily. Of course, her face and whiskers needed extra washing – cod-liver oil has a strong fishy smell – but the treatment worked, and the bitch was able to continue her show career, and went on to become a Champion.

EXTERNAL PARASITES
Even the cleanest dog can occasionally pick up a flea. If left untreated, in a very short space of time the dog will be scratching frantically. Black, gritty specks in the coat indicate the presence of fleas. Lice and ticks can also be unwelcome visitors. Luckily, there are many quick and effective treatments, including one which can be given orally, available from your vet to rid dogs of these parasites.

GRASS SEEDS
These are a summer and early autumn hazard for the country dog. The seeds can penetrate the skin and feet, and, if neglected, they may have to be surgically removed.

HEAT AND SUNSTROKE
Shih Tzus are sometimes affected by hot weather and can suffer from sunstroke. If your dog starts to pant and salivate excessively, you must act quickly to prevent him collapsing. Apply cold water and ice, and soak him to the skin if necessary. In the hot weather, make sure you keep a cool-bag, packed with wet towels and ice, in the car. Always remember that a dog should not be left alone in a locked car. Even on quite a cool day the interior of a parked car heats up very quickly, and on a hot day it becomes a death trap in a very short space of time. Every year dogs die because their owners do not realise that it is dangerous to leave their pet shut in a hot car.

INOCULATIONS
The injections which the young puppy had as protection against distemper, hepatitis, leptospirosis, and parvovirus, need a booster injection yearly to keep the dog safe from these diseases. Britain is rabies free, but in many other countries a dog is also required to have regular rabies injections.

LIMPING
Check paws for cuts or foreign objects (gravel, glass, grass seed, etc.) between the pads. Feel along the affected limb, the dog will react if you touch the injured spot. A slight strain will often respond to rest. Veterinary attention is usually needed for a lame dog.

Your Shih Tzu will need an annual booster inoculation throughout his life to protect him against the major contagious diseases.

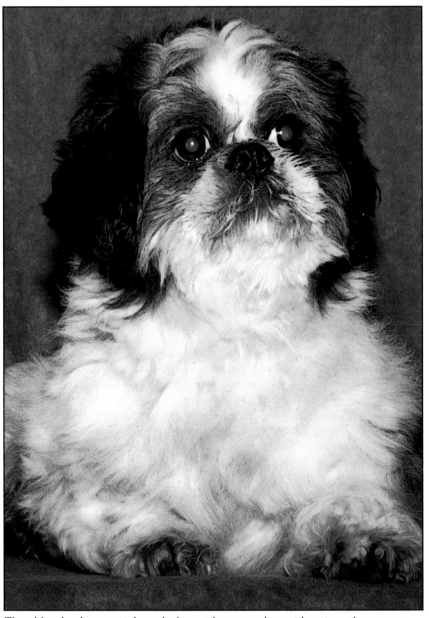

The older dog has special needs, but with care and consideration, the veteran Shih Tzu will enjoy the last years of his life to the full.

MISALLIANCE

Not strictly a health problem, but occasionally a bitch will get herself mated by an unsuitable male. The owner may decide to let the bitch have a litter of puppies, and it is usually quite easy to find homes for pretty crossbred or mixed breed puppies. However, there may be good reasons why a litter is not wanted; in which case, prompt action is needed. Take the bitch to your veterinary surgeon straight away, and he can give her an injection to stop a possible pregnancy.

OBESITY

It is very easy for a family pet to over-eat, especially if he is allowed have scraps from the dining table in addition to his own food. Some Shih Tzus are very greedy, and will eat everything in sight. A healthy dog should have a firm covering of flesh – not layers of fat. If necessary, put your dog on a diet. Remember that too much weight will put a strain on the heart.

SCRATCHING

This is not only unpleasant for the dog, but will quickly ruin a Shih Tzu's beautiful coat. This problem is sometimes caused by incorrect diet, so change to white meat (chicken or rabbit) and feed brown rice in place of biscuit meal. If you are feeding a complete food, change to a rice and chicken recipe food. Milk of Magnesia sometimes helps to cool the dog's blood. If the dog has dry skin, add a few drops of corn-oil to his food.

TEETH

Dogs, like humans, can have problems with their teeth. If you give your Shih Tzu a hard nylon bone to play with, it will help to keep his teeth clean. If your dog starts to pick at his food, and rubs his jaw against the furniture – sometimes quietly moaning – he is almost certainly suffering from toothache. A visit to the veterinary surgeon will confirm what needs to be done. The removal of decaying teeth will often give an elderly dog fresh enjoyment of his food.

TEMPERATURE

The normal temperature for a dog is 101 degrees Fahrenheit (38.3 degrees Centigrade), and as mentioned in Chapter Eight, a bitch's temperature will drop some twelve hours before she whelps. To take a dog's temperature, a greased clinical thermometer is inserted into the rectum, and held there for thirty to sixty seconds. It is easier if two people are involved, one to hold the dog still, while the other actually uses the thermometer. After use, the thermometer must be cleaned and disinfected, and the mercury shaken back down to around 97 F (36 C). If the temperature is over 102.5 F, the dog is in need of urgent veterinary attention.

TRAVEL SICKNESS

Some dogs are bad travellers, and vomit or drool heavily when in a moving vehicle. If you are going on a long journey, avoid feeding your dog for several hours before you set off. There are travel sickness tablets available which help with this problem. Be prepared for accidents in the car, and take a supply of kitchen towels to clean up the car, and a damp cloth to wipe the dog's mouth and whiskers.

VOMITING AND DIARRHOEA

Occasionally a dog will eat something which disagrees with him, causing vomiting and diarrhoea. Fresh raw garlic is a good internal disinfectant, and a small piece of garlic mashed with butter or margarine will slip down a Shih Tzu's throat quite easily. It is advisable to starve your dog for twenty-four hours, making sure that fresh water is available at all times– to give the stomach a chance to recover. If the sickness and diarrhoea does not clear up quickly, consult your veterinary surgeon.

WORMS

Dogs are sometimes unwilling hosts to worms. The most common kind in puppies and young dogs is the roundworm, but from time to time a dog can also harbour the hookworm, whipworm or tapeworm. It is possible to get worm remedies from pet shops, but it is better to consult your veterinary surgeon. It is advisable to follow a regular worming programme, treating your dog routinely for possible infestation every six months.

HOMOEOPATHIC REMEDIES

I am a firm believer in seeking veterinary expertise if a dog is ill. However, I do keep a stock of homoeopathic remedies for minor and everyday ailments. These remedies are readily available from health food shops. The following are all in my first-aid cupboard:

ACONITE: A useful fever remedy.
ALUMINA: For old dogs with weak muscles; also good for constipation.
ARNICA: Helpful after teeth have been extracted. It also has antiseptic properties. It is possible to get Arnica lotion and ointment for external use.
CONIUM: Helpful for old dogs with weak hindlimbs.
EUPHRASIA: Good for eye problems.
GELSEMIUM: Good for nervousness and shock.
NUX VOM: Give after over-eating unsuitable foods.
RHUS TOX: A rheumatic remedy, also good for pulled muscles.
SULPHUR: A mange remedy, it can also help with scratching.
SYMPHYTUM: The homoeopathic version of the herb Knitbone, promotes healing of fractures, etc.

There are, of course, many other homoeopathic remedies available, and there are a number of homoeopathic veterinary surgeons.

THE VETERAN SHIH TZU

The old dog has special needs, and the owner must ensure that the veteran has all the comforts he requires. Make extra-sure that your Shih Tzu has a warm bed which is out of draughts. An older dog often appreciates two small meals a day – an egg beaten in milk makes an occasional treat. As a dog reaches old age he is often content to potter about the garden, instead of going for walks. However, if your elderly dog is still very active and looks forward to his daily walk, continue to take him. Just keep an eye on him and make sure that he does not get tired. Ask your vet to check the dog's teeth. The removal of decayed teeth often gives the pensioner a new lease of life.

If you own a Shih Tzu, you will be rewarded with a dog who has a rare blend of loving companionship, good humour and mischief in his make-up.

It is unkind to keep an old dog alive if he lacks all quality of life. We all hope that our old favourite will die peacefully in his sleep, but sometimes it is necessary to make the hard decision to ask the veterinary surgeon to help him on his way. Sadly, a dog's lifespan is very short, but always remember the love and devotion your old friend gave you, and the fun you shared during his lifetime.